OLYMPIAD WORKBOOK

INTERNATIONAL ENGLISH OLYMPIAD

01 **Learning Objectives**

02 **Multiple Choice Questions**

03 **HOTS (Achievers Section)**

04 **Model Test Paper**

05 **Answer Keys and Solutions**

06 **OMR Answer Sheet**

V&S PUBLISHERS

Published by:

V&S PUBLISHERS

F-2/16, Ansari road, Daryaganj, New Delhi-110002
☎ 23240026, 23240027 • *Fax:* 011-23240028
✉ info@vspublishers.com • 🌐 www.vspublishers.com

Online Brandstore: amazon.in/vspublishers

Regional Office : Hyderabad
5-1-707/1, Brij Bhawan (Beside Central Bank of India Lane)
Bank Street, Koti, Hyderabad - 500 095
☎ 040-24737290
✉ vspublishershyd@gmail.com

Follow us on:   

BUY OUR BOOKS FROM: | AMAZON | | FLIPKART |

© Copyright: **V&S PUBLISHERS**
ISBN 978-81-978021-3-3
New Edition

DISCLAIMER

PUBLISHER'S NOTE

V&S Publishers has carved a significant niche in the publishing industry over the last decade, having successfully published more than 1000 titles across 9 languages spanning over 50 subject categories. Being known for the quality of content, we have built a reputation of excellence and reliability. We have consistently delivered **"Value & Substance"** to our readers, through a wide range of titles across a variety of genres covering school books, fiction and non-fiction that caters to different people from every section of the society.

The **Olympiad Guidebooks for classes 1-10** across all subjects, launched almost a decade ago, under the **GEN X Imprint**, became a go-to-source for the school students in no time, owing to their invaluable and substantive content written in a guidebook pattern,.

Having successfully sold a million copies of the same and in response to demand by both students as well as shopkeepers nationwide; we now present before you our newly launched **Olympiad Workbook Series**, designed for **classes 1-10 across 4 subjects**.

The workbooks are meticulously curated by a team of experienced educators, researchers and subject matter experts, edited by professionals and peer reviewed by teachers. The team has poured its efforts and expertise into creating a crisp and concise workbook which will help and guide the students to the path of success in Olympiad exams. The **MCQs** identified will not only help in scoring top marks in Olympiads but also inculcate a sense of deeper understanding of the subject, by way of solving **HOTS** and referring to complete solutions at the end of the book.

Here we present our new release– **OLYMPIAD WORKBOOK (IEO) CLASS–10** having following features:

- ☞ Based on the latest syllabi
- ☞ MCQs with comprehensive coverage of topics
- ☞ HOTS Questions liberally included
- ☞ A dedicated chapter on logical reasoning
- ☞ Model test paper for thorough practice
- ☞ Sample OMR sheet for real time simulation

We have made sure through our best efforts, that this workbook strictly follows the latest syllabi and patterns of the Olympiad Examination.

As **V&S Publishers** continuously strive to enhance the readability and maintain the credibility of our academic publications, we seek the support of our valuable readers in influencing and enriching the lives of future generations of students.

P.S. While every care has been taken to ensure the correctness of the content, if you come across any error, howsoever minor, do not hesitate to discuss with teachers while pointing that out to us in no uncertain terms.

We wish you all the best for your exams!

DISTINCTIVE FEATURES

01 — Learning Objectives

They list the whole chapter as subtopics, helping the teachers to guide children in a step-by-step manner.

02 — Multiple Choice Questions

MCQs act as an excellent learning aid, helping you to understand and work on your mistakes.

03 — HOTS (Achievers Section)

The High Order Thinking Questions aim to help the student to solve Application-based questions and gain practical understanding of the subject.

04 — Model Test Paper

Model test paper are provided at the end of each book, which help the student to test the knowledge which they have gained after thorough reading of all chapters.

05 — Answer Key

Detailed Answer Key along with explanations aid the pupil to indentify, understand the mistakes they make during the course of Olympiad preparation.

CONTENTS

SYNONYMS, ANTONYMS, HOMOPHONES AND HOMONYMS

LEARNING OBJECTIVES

➤ Synonyms and Antonyms
➤ Homophones and Homonyms

PRACTICE EXERCISE

I. Choose the correct option to mark the synonym of the words given in the questions.

1. Sage
   (A) Wise man   (B) Era
   (C) Tropical tree   (D) Fool

2. Admonish
   (A) Polish   (B) Distribute
   (C) Escape   (D) Caution

3. Beset
   (A) Plead   (B) Deny
   (C) Perplex   (D) Deprive

4. Figment
   (A) Ornamental openwork
   (B) Perfume
   (C) Invention
   (D) Undeveloped

5. Glib
   (A) Dull   (B) Fluent
   (C) Thin   (D) Sharp

6. Coalesce
   (A) Associate   (B) Conspire
   (C) Combine   (D) Cover

7. Quack
   (A) Clown   (B) Dressmaker
   (C) Philanthropist   (D) Charlatan

8. Gauche
   (A) Clumsy   (B) Impudent
   (C) Stupid   (D) Foreign

9. Redundant
   (A) Necessary   (B) Diminishing
   (C) Plentiful   (D) Superfluous

10. Atrophy
    (A) Wither   (B) Grow
    (C) Soften   (D) Spread

11. Vehement
    (A) Thorough
    (B) Smooth-running
    (C) Airy
    (D) Forceful

12. Remuneration
    (A) Understanding   (B) Protest
    (C) Finality   (D) Compensation

13. Frivolity
    (A) Lightness   (B) Ornamentation
    (C) Irritability   (D) Impurity

14. Aura
    (A) Bitterness
    (B) Prophet
    (C) Delight
    (D) Distinctive atmosphere

15. Personable
    (A) Self-centred
    (B) Intimate
    (C) Attractive
    (D) Sensitive

16. Resilience
    (A) Submission
    (B) Determination
    (C) Elasticity
    (D) Recovery

17. Analogy
    (A) Similarity
    (B) Distinction
    (C) Transposition
    (D) Variety

18. Facetious
    (A) Obscene
    (B) Complimentary
    (C) Shrewd
    (D) Witty

19. Diatribe
    (A) Debate
    (B) Tirade
    (C) Monologue
    (D) Oration

20. Malediction
    (A) Curse
    (B) Tactless remark
    (C) Epitaph
    (D) Grammatical error

21. Turbulence
    (A) Treachery
    (B) Triumph
    (C) Commotion
    (D) Overflow

22. Defer
    (A) Discourage
    (B) Minimize
    (C) Postpone
    (D) Estimate

23. Adage
    (A) Proverb
    (B) Youth
    (C) Supplement
    (D) Hardness

24. Ensue
    (A) Compel
    (B) Plead
    (C) Remain
    (D) Follow

25. Zenith
    (A) Lowest Point
    (B) Middle
    (C) Compass
    (D) Summit

26. Hypothetical
    (A) Magical
    (B) Theoretical
    (C) Visual
    (D) Two-faced

27. Superficial
    (A) Shallow
    (B) Aged
    (C) Unusually fine
    (D) Proud

28. Disparage
    (A) Separate
    (B) Belittle
    (C) Compare
    (D) Imitate

29. Protagonist
    (A) Prophet
    (B) Convert
    (C) Explorer
    (D) Champion

30. Impromptu
    (A) Offhand
    (B) Rehearsed
    (C) Laughable
    (D) Deceptive

Select a suitable synonym from the given options.

31. Entice
    - (A) Inform
    - (B) Attract
    - (C) Observe
    - (D) Disobey

32. Acclaim
    - (A) Discharge
    - (B) Divide
    - (C) Excel
    - (D) Applaud

33. Stilted
    - (A) Artificial
    - (B) Fashionable
    - (C) Canonical
    - (D) Senseless

44. Soliloquy
    - (A) Figure of speech
    - (B) Isolated position
    - (C) Historical Incident
    - (D) Monologue

Direction for 5: Fill in the blanks with the words opposite in meaning to those underlined.

35. What looks like a convenient shortcut may prove to be very ______________ in the long run.

1. Ⓐ Ⓑ Ⓒ Ⓓ	8. Ⓐ Ⓑ Ⓒ Ⓓ	15. Ⓐ Ⓑ Ⓒ Ⓓ	22 Ⓐ Ⓑ Ⓒ Ⓓ	29. Ⓐ Ⓑ Ⓒ Ⓓ
2. Ⓐ Ⓑ Ⓒ Ⓓ	9. Ⓐ Ⓑ Ⓒ Ⓓ	16. Ⓐ Ⓑ Ⓒ Ⓓ	23. Ⓐ Ⓑ Ⓒ Ⓓ	30. Ⓐ Ⓑ Ⓒ Ⓓ
3. Ⓐ Ⓑ Ⓒ Ⓓ	10. Ⓐ Ⓑ Ⓒ Ⓓ	17. Ⓐ Ⓑ Ⓒ Ⓓ	24. Ⓐ Ⓑ Ⓒ Ⓓ	31. Ⓐ Ⓑ Ⓒ Ⓓ
4. Ⓐ Ⓑ Ⓒ Ⓓ	11. Ⓐ Ⓑ Ⓒ Ⓓ	18. Ⓐ Ⓑ Ⓒ Ⓓ	25. Ⓐ Ⓑ Ⓒ Ⓓ	32. Ⓐ Ⓑ Ⓒ Ⓓ
5. Ⓐ Ⓑ Ⓒ Ⓓ	12. Ⓐ Ⓑ Ⓒ Ⓓ	19. Ⓐ Ⓑ Ⓒ Ⓓ	26. Ⓐ Ⓑ Ⓒ Ⓓ	33. Ⓐ Ⓑ Ⓒ Ⓓ
6. Ⓐ Ⓑ Ⓒ Ⓓ	13. Ⓐ Ⓑ Ⓒ Ⓓ	20. Ⓐ Ⓑ Ⓒ Ⓓ	27. Ⓐ Ⓑ Ⓒ Ⓓ	34. Ⓐ Ⓑ Ⓒ Ⓓ
7. Ⓐ Ⓑ Ⓒ Ⓓ	14. Ⓐ Ⓑ Ⓒ Ⓓ	21. Ⓐ Ⓑ Ⓒ Ⓓ	28. Ⓐ Ⓑ Ⓒ Ⓓ	35. Ⓐ Ⓑ Ⓒ Ⓓ

SPELLING, ANALOGY AND COLLOCATIONS

PRACTICE EXERCISE

VIII. Select the correct option in order to complete the analogy.

1. Doctor : Nurse :: ? : Follower
   (A) Employer
   (B) Leader
   (C) Worker
   (D) Manager

2. Moon : Satellite :: Earth : ?
   (A) Sun
   (B) Planet
   (C) Solar System
   (D) Asteroid

3. Fear : Threat :: Anger : ?
   (A) Compulsion
   (B) Panic
   (C) Provocation
   (D) Force

4. Clock : Time :: Thermometer : ?
   (A) Heat
   (B) Radiation
   (C) Energy
   (D) Temperature

5. Cup : Lip :: Bird : ?
   (A) Bush
   (B) Grass
   (C) Forest
   (D) Beak

6. Tractor : Trailer :: Horse : ?
   (A) Stable
   (B) Cart
   (C) Saddle
   (D) Engine

7. Flower : Bud :: Plant : ?
   (A) Twig
   (B) Seed
   (C) Taste
   (D) Flower

8. Flow : River :: Stagnant : ?
   (A) Rain
   (B) Stream
   (C) Pool
   (D) Canal

9. Paw : Cat :: Hoof : ?
   (A) Lamb
   (B) Horse
   (C) Elephant
   (D) Lion

10. Car : Garage :: Aeroplane : ?
    (A) Port
    (B) Depot
    (C) Hangar
    (D) Harbour

11. Venerate : Worship :: Extol : ?
    (A) Glorify
    (B) Homage
    (C) Compliment
    (D) Recommend

12. Nurture : Neglect :: Denigrate : ?
    (A) Reveal
    (B) Extol
    (C) Recognise
    (D) Caluminate
13. Hong Kong : China :: Vatican : ?
    (A) Rome
    (B) Mexico
    (C) Canada
    (D) Australia
14. Illiteracy : Education :: Flood : ?
    (A) Rain
    (B) Bridge
    (C) Dam
    (D) River
15. Hill : Mountain :: Stream : ?
    (A) River
    (B) Canal
    (C) Glacier
    (D) Avalanche
16. Fruit : Banana :: Mammal : ?
    (A) Cow   (B) Snake
    (C) Fish   (D) Sparrow
17. Fire : Ashes :: Explosion : ?
    (A) Flame   (B) Debris
    (C) Sound   (D) Death
18. Drama : Stage :: Tennis : ?
    (A) Net   (B) Tournament
    (C) Racket   (D) Court
19. Sculptor : Statue :: Poet : ?
    (A) Canvas   (B) Pen
    (C) Verse   (D) Chisel
20. Malaria : Disease :: Spear : ?
    (A) Wound
    (B) Sword
    (C) Weapon
    (D) Death
21. Reading : Knowledge :: Work : ?
    (A) Experience
    (B) Engagement
    (C) Employment
    (D) Experiment
22. Cricket : Bat :: Hockey : ?

23. Enough : Excess :: Sufficiency : ?
    (A) Field
    (B) Stick
    (C) Player
    (D) Ball
23. Enough : Excess :: Sufficiency : ?
    (A) Adequacy
    (B) Surplus
    (C) Competency
    (D) Import
24. Skeleton : Body :: Grammar : ?
    (A) Language
    (B) Sentence
    (C) Meaning
    (D) Education
25. Mature : Regressed :: Varied : ?
    (A) Rhythmic
    (B) Monotonous
    (C) Decorous
    (D) Obsolete
26. Ship : Sea :: Camel : ?
    (A) Forest
    (B) Land
    (C) Mountain
    (D) Desert
27. Dilatory : Expeditious :: Direct : ?
    (A) Tortuous
    (B) Circumlocutory
    (C) Straight
    (D) Curved
28. Wrist : Elbow :: Ankle : ?
    (A) Heel
    (B) Fingers
    (C) Foot
    (D) Knee
29. Amber : Yellow :: Caramine : ?
    (A) Red
    (B) Green
    (C) Violet
    (D) Blue
30. Wax : Wane :: Zenith : ?
    (A) Nadir
    (B) Bottom
    (C) Fall
    (D) Height

Direction 1-5: Select the pair among the given choices which is related in the same way as the words given in CAPITAL letters.

31. REPROACH : APPROVAL :: ?
    (A) Sorcery : Black magic
    (B) Disapprove : Disgrace
    (C) Stupendous : Gigantic
    (D) Svelte : Obese
    (E) None of these

32. AUGUR : FUTURE :: ?
    (A) Knight : Medieval
    (B) Poet : Century
    (C) Vanguard : Pack
    (D) Historian : Past
    (E) None of these

33. GARBAGE : SQUALOR :: ?
    (A) Colour : Brush
    (B) Dirt: Cleanliness
    (C) Diamond : Magnificence
    (D) Poor : Hunger
    (E) None of these

34. IRK : APPEASE :: ?
    (A) Appreciate : Deprave
    (B) Quibble : Clarify
    (C) Ridicule : Decorate
    (D) Stupefy : Debilitate

35. WIND : GALE :: ?
    (A) Disaster : Calamity
    (B) Storm : Sea
    (C) Love : Passion
    (D) Disgust : Infatuation

—Darken Your Choice with HB Pencil—

1. Ⓐ Ⓑ Ⓒ Ⓓ	8. Ⓐ Ⓑ Ⓒ Ⓓ	15. Ⓐ Ⓑ Ⓒ Ⓓ	22. Ⓐ Ⓑ Ⓒ Ⓓ	29. Ⓐ Ⓑ Ⓒ Ⓓ
2. Ⓐ Ⓑ Ⓒ Ⓓ	9. Ⓐ Ⓑ Ⓒ Ⓓ	16. Ⓐ Ⓑ Ⓒ Ⓓ	23. Ⓐ Ⓑ Ⓒ Ⓓ	30. Ⓐ Ⓑ Ⓒ Ⓓ
3. Ⓐ Ⓑ Ⓒ Ⓓ	10. Ⓐ Ⓑ Ⓒ Ⓓ	17. Ⓐ Ⓑ Ⓒ Ⓓ	24. Ⓐ Ⓑ Ⓒ Ⓓ	31. Ⓐ Ⓑ Ⓒ Ⓓ
4. Ⓐ Ⓑ Ⓒ Ⓓ	11. Ⓐ Ⓑ Ⓒ Ⓓ	18. Ⓐ Ⓑ Ⓒ Ⓓ	25. Ⓐ Ⓑ Ⓒ Ⓓ	32. Ⓐ Ⓑ Ⓒ Ⓓ
5. Ⓐ Ⓑ Ⓒ Ⓓ	12. Ⓐ Ⓑ Ⓒ Ⓓ	19. Ⓐ Ⓑ Ⓒ Ⓓ	26. Ⓐ Ⓑ Ⓒ Ⓓ	33. Ⓐ Ⓑ Ⓒ Ⓓ
6. Ⓐ Ⓑ Ⓒ Ⓓ	13. Ⓐ Ⓑ Ⓒ Ⓓ	20. Ⓐ Ⓑ Ⓒ Ⓓ	27. Ⓐ Ⓑ Ⓒ Ⓓ	34. Ⓐ Ⓑ Ⓒ Ⓓ
7. Ⓐ Ⓑ Ⓒ Ⓓ	14. Ⓐ Ⓑ Ⓒ Ⓓ	21. Ⓐ Ⓑ Ⓒ Ⓓ	28. Ⓐ Ⓑ Ⓒ Ⓓ	35. Ⓐ Ⓑ Ⓒ Ⓓ

ONE WORD AND IDIOMS

LEARNING OBJECTIVES

➤ Concept of One Word substitution
➤ Basic of Idioms

PRACTICE EXERCISE

I. Choose the correct option that best explains the given word.

1. Altruist
   - (A) One who is lover of beauty.
   - (B) One who never stops.
   - (C) A lover of mankind.
   - (D) A person who hates mankind.

2. Amateur
   - (A) One who is not having experience.
   - (B) One who does a thing for pleasure and not as a profession.
   - (C) One who have all happiness.
   - (D) One who remains sad.

3. Ambidextrous
   - (A) Person who can eat veg and non veg.
   - (B) One who feeds on flesh
   - (C) One who can use either hand with ease.
   - (D) None of the above.

4. Anarchist
   - (A) Religious person.
   - (B) Person against a particular religion.
   - (C) Person who always suspects.
   - (D) One who is out to destroy all governments, peace and order

5. Arbitrator
   - (A) A person appointed by two parties to solve a dispute
   - (B) A person who is appointed to give punishment
   - (C) A person who is always aggressive
   - (D) A person who always give blessings

6. Ascetic
   - (A) One who is in confusion
   - (B) One who make paintings
   - (C) One who leads an austere life
   - (D) One who is lover of beauty

7. Bohemian
   - (A) Waves in the sea
   - (B) Fresh mood
   - (C) Irritation
   - (D) An unconventional style of living

8. Cacographist
   - (A) One who is having ego
   - (B) One who has unique style
   - (C) One who is bad in spelling
   - (D) One who is good in spelling

9. Chauvinist
   (A) A person displaying aggressive or exaggerated patriotism
   (B) A person showing disappointment
   (C) A person feeling low
   (D) A person feeling very excited

10. Connoisseur
   (A) An ideal   (B) A participant
   (C) An expert judge   (D) A beautiful girl

11. Contemporaries
   (A) A type dance.
   (B) A person or thing, living or existing at the same time.
   (C) Angry mob.
   (D) A type of protest.

12. Convalescent
   (A) One who is always obeyed.
   (B) One who gets whatever he desires.
   (C) One who have lost his loved one.
   (D) Recovering from an illness or operation.

13. Coquette
   (A) A motivational lady.
   (B) A woman who flirts.
   (C) A woman who can protect herself.
   (D) None of the above.

14. Cosmopolitan
   (A) A person who can speak all languages.
   (B) A person who regards the whole world as his country.
   (C) A person who is having knowledge of all topics.
   (D) None of the above.

15. Cynosure
   (A) One who always remains happy.
   (B) One who is not present.
   (C) One who is hated by everyone.
   (D) One who is centre of attraction.

16. Cynic
   (A) One who sneers at the beliefs of others.
   (B) One who appreciates.
   (C) One who is confused.
   (D) One who is candidate for something.

17. Debonair
   (A) Suave.
   (B) Irritated.
   (C) Calm.
   (D) None of the above.

II. Choose the correct meaning of the given proverb/idiom. If there is no correct meaning given, i.e. 'None of these' will be the answer.

18. To make clean breast of
   (A) To gain prominence
   (B) To praise oneself
   (C) To confess without of reserve
   (D) To destroy before it blooms
   (E) None of these

19. To keep one's temper
   (A) To become hungry
   (B) To be in good mood
   (C) To preserve ones energy
   (D) To be aloof from
   (E) None of these

20. To catch a tartar
   (A) To trap wanted criminal with great difficulty
   (B) To catch a dangerous person
   (C) To meet with disaster
   (D) To deal with a person who is more than one's match
   (E) None of these

21. To drive home
    (A) To find one's roots
    (B) To return to place of rest
    (C) Back to original position
    (D) To emphasise
    (E) None of these

22. To have an axe to grind
    (A) A private end to serve
    (B) To fail to arouse interest
    (C) To have no result
    (D) To work for both sides
    (E) None of these

23. To cry wolf
    (A) To listen eagerly
    (B) To give false alarm
    (C) To turn pale
    (D) To keep off starvation
    (E) None of these

24. To end in smoke
    (A) To make completely understand
    (B) To ruin oneself
    (C) To excite great applause
    (D) To overcome someone
    (E) None of these

25. To be above board
    (A) To have a good height
    (B) To be honest in any business deal
    (C) They have no debts
    (D) To try to be beautiful
    (E) None of these

26. To put one's hand to plough
    (A) To take up agricultural farming
    (B) To take a difficult task
    (C) To get entangled into unnecessary things
    (D) Take interest in technical work
    (E) None of these

27. To pick holes
    (A) To find some reason to quarrel
    (B) To destroy something
    (C) To criticise someone
    (D) To cut some part of an item
    (E) None of these

28. To smell a rat
    (A) To see signs of plague epidemic
    (B) To get bad small of a bad dead rat
    (C) To suspect foul dealings
    (D) To be in a bad mood
    (E) None of these

29. To hit the nail right on the head
    (A) To do the right thing
    (B) To destroy one's reputation
    (C) To announce one's fixed views
    (D) To teach someone a lesson
    (E) None of these

30. To set one's face against
    (A) To oppose with determination
    (B) To judge by appearance
    (C) To get out of difficulty
    (D) To look at one steadily
    (E) None of these

31. Chemistry in ancient times is called
    (A) Anatomy   (B) Alchemy
    (C) Bibliography   (D) Anthropology
32. The study of plants is called
    (A) Bacteriology   (B) Astrology
    (C) Arboriculture   (D) Botany
33. The study of human population with the help of the records of the number of births and deaths is called
    (A) Ecology   (B) Demography
    (C) Entomology   (D) Epigraphy

Select the option with the correct usage/ meaning of the word/phrase.

34.

	Dictionary definition		Usage
A	Adequately and properly aged so as to be free of harshness	E	He has mellowed with age
B	Freed from the rashness of youth	F	The tones of the old violin were mellow
C	Of soft and loamy consistency	G	Some wines are mellow.
D	Rich and pleasant	H	Mellow soil is found in the Gangetic plains.

A. A-E, B-G, C-F, D-H
B. A-E, B F, C-G, D-H
C. A G, B E, C-H, D-F
D. A-H, B-G, C-F, D-E

35.

	Dictionary definition		Usage
A	Remove a stigma from the name of	E	The opposition was purged after the coup.
B	Make clean by removing whatever is superfluous, foreign	F	The committee heard his attempt to purge himself of a charge of heresy
C	Get rid of	G	Drugs that purge the bowels are often bad for the brain.
D	To cause evacuation of	H	It is recommended to purge water by distillation

A. A-E, B-G, C-F, D-H
B. A-F, B-E, C-G, D-H
C. A-H, B-F, C-G, D-E
D. A-F, B-H, C-E, D-G

—Darken Your Choice with HB Pencil—

1. Ⓐ Ⓑ Ⓒ Ⓓ	8. Ⓐ Ⓑ Ⓒ Ⓓ	15. Ⓐ Ⓑ Ⓒ Ⓓ	22. Ⓐ Ⓑ Ⓒ Ⓓ	29. Ⓐ Ⓑ Ⓒ Ⓓ
2. Ⓐ Ⓑ Ⓒ Ⓓ	9. Ⓐ Ⓑ Ⓒ Ⓓ	16. Ⓐ Ⓑ Ⓒ Ⓓ	23. Ⓐ Ⓑ Ⓒ Ⓓ	30. Ⓐ Ⓑ Ⓒ Ⓓ
3. Ⓐ Ⓑ Ⓒ Ⓓ	10. Ⓐ Ⓑ Ⓒ Ⓓ	17. Ⓐ Ⓑ Ⓒ Ⓓ	24. Ⓐ Ⓑ Ⓒ Ⓓ	31. Ⓐ Ⓑ Ⓒ Ⓓ
4. Ⓐ Ⓑ Ⓒ Ⓓ	11. Ⓐ Ⓑ Ⓒ Ⓓ	18. Ⓐ Ⓑ Ⓒ Ⓓ	25. Ⓐ Ⓑ Ⓒ Ⓓ	32. Ⓐ Ⓑ Ⓒ Ⓓ
5. Ⓐ Ⓑ Ⓒ Ⓓ	12. Ⓐ Ⓑ Ⓒ Ⓓ	19. Ⓐ Ⓑ Ⓒ Ⓓ	26. Ⓐ Ⓑ Ⓒ Ⓓ	33. Ⓐ Ⓑ Ⓒ Ⓓ
6. Ⓐ Ⓑ Ⓒ Ⓓ	13. Ⓐ Ⓑ Ⓒ Ⓓ	20. Ⓐ Ⓑ Ⓒ Ⓓ	27. Ⓐ Ⓑ Ⓒ Ⓓ	34. Ⓐ Ⓑ Ⓒ Ⓓ
7. Ⓐ Ⓑ Ⓒ Ⓓ	14. Ⓐ Ⓑ Ⓒ Ⓓ	21. Ⓐ Ⓑ Ⓒ Ⓓ	28. Ⓐ Ⓑ Ⓒ Ⓓ	35. Ⓐ Ⓑ Ⓒ Ⓓ

ERROR IN SENTENCE AND SENTENCE SEQUENCING

LEARNING OBJECTIVES

➤ Error in sentences/phrases
➤ Sentence Sequencing

PRACTICE EXERCISE

See the following sentences/phrases and chose the one with an error.

1. His comments are just (A)/ abstract theory and show (B)/ little understanding of the realities of the situation. (C)
   (A) A
   (B) B
   (C) C
   (D) No error

2. The only thing (A)/ wealth does for (B)/ some people is to make (C)/ them worry about loosing them. (D)
   (A) A
   (B) B
   (C) C
   (D) D

3. The attention of the (A)/ investigators were drawn (B)/ to the fact that, the door (C)/ of one of the houses was open. (D)
   (A) A
   (B) C, D
   (C) B
   (D) A, C

4. Two hours after its (A)/ take-off, the flight reached (B)/ Mumbai Airport, when (C)/ it stopped for a short interval (D)
   (A) A
   (B) D
   (C) B
   (D) C

5. If there was less (A)/ sympathy in the world, (B)/ there would be less (C)/ trouble in the world. (D)
   (A) A
   (B) B
   (C) C
   (D) D

6. Based on the images they see in (A) advertisements, women often feel that they should be thin (B) and beautiful and hold on full-time jobs while (C) also being full-time mothers. (D)
   (A) A
   (B) B
   (C) C
   (D) D

7. Advertisements for many sugary cereals (A) encourage children to ask their parents (B) for those particular products regardless whether (C) the products are good for them (D)
   (A) A
   (B) B
   (C) C
   (D) D

8. Fields which require the relaxation in FDI restrictions include (A) civil aviation, construction development, industrial parks, (B) petroleum and natural gas, commodity exchanges, (C) credit-information services and mining. (D)
   (A) A
   (B) B
   (C) C
   (D) D

9. The problem arises when the dramatization (A) crossed the line by falsely representing a product (B) and hefty fines can result from false advertising (C) when levied by the Federal Trade Commission. (D)
   (A) A
   (B) B
   (C) C
   (D) D

10. The anti-global sentiment was a key part (A) of Trump's election campaign, and his (B) short time in office has shown willingness to talk (C) about changing the way the U.S. trades with the world. (D)

(A) A
(B) B
(C) C
(D) D

Direction: Read the following sentences and identify and correct the errors.

11. Many peoples attended the funeral of the great man.

12. The shepherd took the cattles to the field.

13. Sita could not understands what the teacher was saying.

14. Do you know the importance for clean water?

15. Laugh is the best medicines.

16. The flock of sheeps blocked the road.

17. The children was playing in the Giant's garden.

18. The children decided to surprise Miss Holmes on teacher's day.

19. I saw Richard when I'm on the flight.

20. Man have depended on nature for a long time.

21. Ramu is a honest man.

22. Bread and butter are Sheldon's favourite breakfast.

23. Birds of feathers flock together.

24. The teacher called me on 12 o'clock.

25. The sweets was distributed between all the children.

HOTS (ACHIEVERS SECTION)

Read the following passage, identify the errors and correct them.

My little sister Lisa was practicing how to riding a bicycle yesterday. Suddenly I hear a loud crash and ran to see what had happened. I saw that she was lying in the ground. I quickly pulled her up and bought her home. She was crying out loud. I quickly go inside the house and brought the first aid box. After cleaning the wound, I apply antiseptic to the wound. Lisa has scratches on her hand and knee. To calm her down, I took her to the nearby shop and brought her a big chocolate. Seeing her favourite chocolate, she immediately stop crying. Within two day, her wounds healed, and she went to play again.

1. Ⓐ Ⓑ Ⓒ Ⓓ	6. Ⓐ Ⓑ Ⓒ Ⓓ	11. Ⓐ Ⓑ Ⓒ Ⓓ	16 Ⓐ Ⓑ Ⓒ Ⓓ	21. Ⓐ Ⓑ Ⓒ Ⓓ
2. Ⓐ Ⓑ Ⓒ Ⓓ	7. Ⓐ Ⓑ Ⓒ Ⓓ	12. Ⓐ Ⓑ Ⓒ Ⓓ	17. Ⓐ Ⓑ Ⓒ Ⓓ	22. Ⓐ Ⓑ Ⓒ Ⓓ
3. Ⓐ Ⓑ Ⓒ Ⓓ	8. Ⓐ Ⓑ Ⓒ Ⓓ	13. Ⓐ Ⓑ Ⓒ Ⓓ	18. Ⓐ Ⓑ Ⓒ Ⓓ	23. Ⓐ Ⓑ Ⓒ Ⓓ
4. Ⓐ Ⓑ Ⓒ Ⓓ	9. Ⓐ Ⓑ Ⓒ Ⓓ	14. Ⓐ Ⓑ Ⓒ Ⓓ	19. Ⓐ Ⓑ Ⓒ Ⓓ	24. Ⓐ Ⓑ Ⓒ Ⓓ
5. Ⓐ Ⓑ Ⓒ Ⓓ	10. Ⓐ Ⓑ Ⓒ Ⓓ	15. Ⓐ Ⓑ Ⓒ Ⓓ	20. Ⓐ Ⓑ Ⓒ Ⓓ	25. Ⓐ Ⓑ Ⓒ Ⓓ

NOUN

LEARNING OBJECTIVES

➤ Types of Noun
➤ Uses of Noun

MULTIPLE CHOICE QUESTIONS

I. Identify whether the underlined nouns are common or proper.

1. My <u>sister</u> is a doctor.
2. A <u>teacher</u> must have patience.
3. The first game of basketball was played in <u>Massachusetts</u>.
4. I didn't believe the <u>girl's</u> story.
5. He worked at the <u>YMCA Training School</u>.
6. Not all cricketers in this team are <u>Indians</u>.
7. James is a bright <u>student</u>.
8. He went to a college in <u>Seattle</u>.
9. <u>Solomon</u> was famous for his wisdom.
10. A <u>player</u> must not run with the ball.

II. Write whether the underlined nouns are countable or uncountable.

11. I drink <u>milk</u> twice a day.
12. My mother puts <u>butter</u> on my bread slices.
13. Today traffic <u>policemen</u> are organizing a traffic awareness event.
14. Can you give me some <u>juice</u> please?
15. I have finished my <u>exercises</u>.
16. I have already filled up five <u>buckets</u> with water.
17. In summers, you should drink lots of <u>water</u> to avoid dehydration.
18. Only qualified <u>candidates</u> are allowed to attend this seminar.
19. My mother prepares delicious <u>bread</u>.
20. There's a hike in the price of <u>oil</u>.

I. Fill in the blanks with the noun form of the words provided.

21. Please take the teacher's ___________ (permit) to participate in NCC.

22. It is my firm ___________ (believe) that you will win the match.

23. Her English is very bad. She must make ___________ (improve)

24. The witness can provide lot of ___________ (inform) about the incident.

25. I find ___________ (happy) in small things of life.

1.	Ⓐ Ⓑ Ⓒ Ⓓ	6.	Ⓐ Ⓑ Ⓒ Ⓓ	11.	Ⓐ Ⓑ Ⓒ Ⓓ	16	Ⓐ Ⓑ Ⓒ Ⓓ	21.	Ⓐ Ⓑ Ⓒ Ⓓ
2.	Ⓐ Ⓑ Ⓒ Ⓓ	7.	Ⓐ Ⓑ Ⓒ Ⓓ	12.	Ⓐ Ⓑ Ⓒ Ⓓ	17.	Ⓐ Ⓑ Ⓒ Ⓓ	22.	Ⓐ Ⓑ Ⓒ Ⓓ
3.	Ⓐ Ⓑ Ⓒ Ⓓ	8.	Ⓐ Ⓑ Ⓒ Ⓓ	13.	Ⓐ Ⓑ Ⓒ Ⓓ	18.	Ⓐ Ⓑ Ⓒ Ⓓ	23.	Ⓐ Ⓑ Ⓒ Ⓓ
4.	Ⓐ Ⓑ Ⓒ Ⓓ	9.	Ⓐ Ⓑ Ⓒ Ⓓ	14.	Ⓐ Ⓑ Ⓒ Ⓓ	19.	Ⓐ Ⓑ Ⓒ Ⓓ	24.	Ⓐ Ⓑ Ⓒ Ⓓ
5.	Ⓐ Ⓑ Ⓒ Ⓓ	10.	Ⓐ Ⓑ Ⓒ Ⓓ	15.	Ⓐ Ⓑ Ⓒ Ⓓ	20.	Ⓐ Ⓑ Ⓒ Ⓓ	25.	Ⓐ Ⓑ Ⓒ Ⓓ

VERBS, ADVERBS, PHRASAL VERBS AND MODALS

LEARNING OBJECTIVES

- ➤ Finite and Non-finite Verbs
- ➤ Uses of Verbs
- ➤ Uses of Modal Verbs
- ➤ Adverbs and their types
- ➤ Phrasal Verbs

PRACTICE EXERCISE

I. Fill in the blanks with the correct option.

1. Carlos is an excellent student. He _________ goes to class.
   - (A) always
   - (B) usually
   - (C) sometimes
   - (D) seldom
   - (E) never

2. I hate vegetables. I _________ eat carrots.
   - (A) always
   - (B) usually
   - (C) sometimes
   - (D) seldom
   - (E) never

3. Robert goes to the gym only two or three times a year. He _________ goes to the gym.
   - (A) always
   - (B) never
   - (C) usually
   - (D) seldom

4. Harold never leaves the college on Friday. He _________ eats at the cafeteria on Fridays.
   - (A) always
   - (B) never
   - (C) seldom

5. Ms. Biethan is always in a good mood. She is _________ sad.
   - (A) always
   - (B) usually
   - (C) never

6. Teresa is not a pleasant person. She is _________ in a bad mood.
   - (A) never
   - (B) seldom
   - (C) always

7. My sister usually drives to work with a friend. She _________ drives alone.
   - (A) never
   - (B) always
   - (C) usually
   - (D) seldom

8. I never lend money to Curtis. He _________ pays me back.
   - (A) sometimes
   - (B) always
   - (C) never
   - (D) usually

9. Susan goes to the beach whenever she can. She _________ misses a chance to go to the ocean.
   - (A) never
   - (B) always
   - (C) usually

10. It almost always rains in Seattle. The sun _________ shines there.
    - (A) always
    - (B) usually
    - (C) seldom

II. Select the right option to fill in the blanks.

11. Could you turn _____ the TV? The soap opera is about to start.
    - (A) back
    - (B) on
    - (C) off
    - (D) out

12. There was nothing good on TV so I turned it _____ and went to bed.
    (A) off
    (B) up
    (C) in
    (D) down

13. The TV is too loud. Can you turn it _____ a bit?
    (A) up
    (B) out
    (C) off
    (D) down

14. The TV is too quiet. Can you turn it _____ a bit?
    (A) back
    (B) off
    (C) up
    (D) over

15. I've been looking _____ my car keys for half an hour. Have you seen them anywhere?
    (A) up
    (B) for
    (C) after
    (D) at

16. My mother has offered to look _____ the children, so we can go to the party.
    (A) for
    (B) into
    (C) at
    (D) after

17. If you don't know what the word means, you'll have to look it _____ in the dictionary.
    (A) for
    (B) up
    (C) out
    (D) off

18. The meeting has been put _____ to Friday as many people have got the flu.
    (A) up
    (B) in
    (C) back
    (D) out

19. The meeting has been brought _____ to Monday due to the seriousness of the situation.
    (A) on
    (B) out
    (C) down
    (D) forward

20. The company is taking _____ new workers to meet this projected demand.
    (A) at
    (B) on
    (C) up
    (D) over

III. Select correct Phrasal verb to fill in the blanks.

21. Has the advertising agency _________ the new promotional material yet? I need it by this afternoon.
    (A) dropped off
    (B) dropped in
    (C) dropped out
    (D) dropped by

22. We need to _________ the price of the product, which is relatively high, and focus on its quality as a selling point.
    (A) back down
    (B) break down
    (C) play down
    (D) settle down

23. Have you _____________ any other interesting product features that we could emphasize in the ads?
    (A) come across
    (B) drawn out
    (C) gotten across
    (D) made out

24. We've decided to _________ billboards and use more double-page spreads instead.
    (A) back off on
    (B) come down with
    (C) cut back on
    (D) drop off

25. This poster is horrible and can't be used. The colours and images are all wrong. We will have to _________ .
    (A) do it over
    (B) even it out
    (C) do it in
    (D) put it down

26. We had to reorder the printed advertisements because the printer completely forgot and _________ the free sample coupons.
    (A) kept off
    (B) left out
    (C) passed out
    (D) shaved off

27. We're going to have to _________ the advertising campaign if we can't get any TV or radio time.
    (A) call on
    (B) call off
    (C) drop off
    (D) drop out

28. This commercial doesn't seem to promote the product. Can you explain to me how dancing chickens __________ sport shoes?
   (A) pan out as   (B) hold up to
   (C) add up to   (D) have to do with

29. I like that magazine, but I think we should __________ advertising in it until its circulation has increased.
   (A) put out   (B) put back
   (C) put away   (D) put off

30. My new assistant needs to be __________ before I trust her to run an ad campaign like this one.
   (A) broken down   (B) broken in
   (C) broken up   (D) broken into

HOTS (ACHIEVERS SECTION)

I. Choose the best phrasal verb to fill in the blanks.

31. It's not such a terrible thing! Don't worry! ______________! (be happy, not be sad).
   (A) cheer up   (B) laugh away
   (C) cheer out   (D) laugh out

32. After being together for twenty years, Paul and Julia ______________ (end a relationship).
   (A) broke down   (B) split off
   (C) broke away   (D) split up

33. I've missed many lessons, so now I'll have to ______________ (reach the same level, learn the same as the others) the other students.
   (A) catch up   (B) catch up with
   (C) hurry up   (D) learn on

34. It's your problem, so try to ________ it ______ (solve).
   (A) work, in   (B) sort, off
   (C) sort, out   (D) solve, in

35. It's too cold in here. Shall I ______________ (increase the temperature) the heating?
   (A) turn on   (B) get up
   (C) turn up   (D) put on

ADJECTIVE

LEARNING OBJECTIVES

➤ Basic concept of Adjectives
➤ Types of Adjectives

PRACTICE EXERCISE

I. Underline the adjectives in the following sentences and identify their type.

1. The car sustained heavy damage in the accident.
2. He has written several stories.
3. A dog is very faithful to its master.
4. Every man has his duties.
5. He is a man of few words.
6. Neither party is quite in the right.
7. Which color do you prefer?
8. The way was long, the wind was cold.
9. He calls me every day.
10. I have not seen him in several days.

II. Fill in the blanks with the correct degree of comparison.

11. She is ………….. than her sister. (pretty)
12. Martha is a ………….. girl. (nice)
13. Supriya is the ………….. girl in the class. (intelligent)
14. Martin speaks English …………... (good)
15. Russia is the ………….. country in the world. (big)
16. China is a ………….. country. (big)
17. China is ………….. than India. (big)
18. This is the ………….. book I have ever read. (interesting)
19. I am ………….. than you. (smart)
20. Take the ………….. of the two routes. (short)

I. Fill in the blanks with suitable adjectives.

21. Tom doesn't take risks when he's driving. He's always ___________.

22. Monica's English is very ___________ although she makes a lot of mistakes.

23. Everything was very quiet. There was ___________ silence.

24. The driver of the car had sustained ___________ injuries.

25. There was a ___________ change in the weather.

Darken Your Choice with HB Pencil

1.	Ⓐ Ⓑ Ⓒ Ⓓ	6.	Ⓐ Ⓑ Ⓒ Ⓓ	11.	Ⓐ Ⓑ Ⓒ Ⓓ	16	Ⓐ Ⓑ Ⓒ Ⓓ	21.	Ⓐ Ⓑ Ⓒ Ⓓ
2.	Ⓐ Ⓑ Ⓒ Ⓓ	7.	Ⓐ Ⓑ Ⓒ Ⓓ	12.	Ⓐ Ⓑ Ⓒ Ⓓ	17.	Ⓐ Ⓑ Ⓒ Ⓓ	22.	Ⓐ Ⓑ Ⓒ Ⓓ
3.	Ⓐ Ⓑ Ⓒ Ⓓ	8.	Ⓐ Ⓑ Ⓒ Ⓓ	13.	Ⓐ Ⓑ Ⓒ Ⓓ	18.	Ⓐ Ⓑ Ⓒ Ⓓ	23.	Ⓐ Ⓑ Ⓒ Ⓓ
4.	Ⓐ Ⓑ Ⓒ Ⓓ	9.	Ⓐ Ⓑ Ⓒ Ⓓ	14.	Ⓐ Ⓑ Ⓒ Ⓓ	19.	Ⓐ Ⓑ Ⓒ Ⓓ	24.	Ⓐ Ⓑ Ⓒ Ⓓ
5.	Ⓐ Ⓑ Ⓒ Ⓓ	10.	Ⓐ Ⓑ Ⓒ Ⓓ	15.	Ⓐ Ⓑ Ⓒ Ⓓ	20.	Ⓐ Ⓑ Ⓒ Ⓓ	25.	Ⓐ Ⓑ Ⓒ Ⓓ

ARTICLES AND PREPOSITIONS 

LEARNING OBJECTIVES

➤ Articles and its Types
➤ Preposition and different Types

PRACTICE EXERCISE

I. Fill in the blanks with the correct preposition.

1. The picture is ____ the wall.
   (A) in   (B) under
   (C) on   (D) at

2. The desks are ____ the blackboard in the classroom.
   (A) opposite   (B) between
   (C) above   (D) behind

3. The cat always sleeps ____ my bed.
   (A) under   (B) above
   (C) between   (D) over

4. The lamp is ____ the table.
   (A) in   (B) above
   (C) on   (D) under

5. The book is ____ the mug and the pen.
   (A) in   (B) between
   (C) on   (D) above

6. There is a bench ____ my house.
   (A) under   (B) on
   (C) in front of   (D) above

7. There are apple trees ____ the house.
   (A) behind   (B) in
   (C) on   (D) at

8. The bookshop is ____ the bank.
   (A) between   (B) above
   (C) next to   (D) over

9. There is a museum ____ the school.
   (A) in   (B) opposite
   (C) under   (D) over

10. There is a bed ____ my room.
    (A) in   (B) on
    (C) under   (D) over

11. The mouse is ____ the cats.
    (A) on   (B) between
    (C) above   (D) over

12. The pillow is ____ the blanket.
    (A) in   (B) between
    (C) under   (D) between

13. The books are ____ my schoolbag.
    (A) above   (B) in
    (C) between   (D) at

14. You sit ____ me in the classroom.
    (A) between   (B) on
    (C) in front of   (D) at

15. My mother's plant is ____ the TV.
    (A) above   (B) in
    (C) in front of   (D) over

16. Mike often hides ____ that tree.
    (A) in   (B) above
    (C) behind   (D) at

17. The computer is ____ the telephone.
   (A) under   (B) next to
   (C) between   (D) on
18. Sam usually sits ____ this chair.
   (A) on   (B) in
   (C) above   (D) over
19. Mary sometimes sits ____ John and Jill.
   (A) between   (B) on
   (C) in front of   (D) over
20. The books are ____ the shelf.
   (A) in   (B) next to
   (C) on   (D) opposite
21. She is gifted ____ common sense.
   (A) on   (B) by
   (C) with   (D) over
22. Sheela burst ____ the room when Mohini was writing a letter.
   (A) on   (B) in
   (C) of   (D) out
23. The players have gone __________ the playground.
   (A) in   (B) over
   (C) with   (D) to
24. He has not met his mother ____ long.
   (A) for   (B) with
   (C) since   (D) by
25. The land was divided ____ the two sisters.
   (A) among   (B) between
   (C) with   (D) for
26. The terrorist shot the policeman ____ his gun.
   (A) by   (B) for
   (C) with   (D) in
27. Compare Gandhi ____ Karl Marx.
   (A) to   (B) with
   (C) over   (D) in.
28. Janardhan was appointed ____ the post of section officer.
   (A) to   (B) on
   (C) with   (D) for
29. My Mother-in-law is blind ____ one eye.
   (A) from   (B) in
   (C) on   (D) of
30. He prevented me ____ going to the school.
   (A) from   (B) for
   (C) with   (D) on

HOTS (ACHIEVERS SECTION)

I. **Fill in the blanks with the suitable article (a/an/the):**

31. I like __________ blue shirt over there better than __________ red one.
32. Carla's father is __________ electrician.
33. I have __________ good idea.
34. Do the Smiths have __________ yellow van?
35. __________ cat, which had entered our kitchen yesterday, had come in again today morning.

——Darken Your Choice with HB Pencil——

1. Ⓐ Ⓑ Ⓒ Ⓓ	8. Ⓐ Ⓑ Ⓒ Ⓓ	15. Ⓐ Ⓑ Ⓒ Ⓓ	22 Ⓐ Ⓑ Ⓒ Ⓓ	29. Ⓐ Ⓑ Ⓒ Ⓓ
2. Ⓐ Ⓑ Ⓒ Ⓓ	9. Ⓐ Ⓑ Ⓒ Ⓓ	16. Ⓐ Ⓑ Ⓒ Ⓓ	23. Ⓐ Ⓑ Ⓒ Ⓓ	30. Ⓐ Ⓑ Ⓒ Ⓓ
3. Ⓐ Ⓑ Ⓒ Ⓓ	10. Ⓐ Ⓑ Ⓒ Ⓓ	17. Ⓐ Ⓑ Ⓒ Ⓓ	24. Ⓐ Ⓑ Ⓒ Ⓓ	31. Ⓐ Ⓑ Ⓒ Ⓓ
4. Ⓐ Ⓑ Ⓒ Ⓓ	11. Ⓐ Ⓑ Ⓒ Ⓓ	18. Ⓐ Ⓑ Ⓒ Ⓓ	25. Ⓐ Ⓑ Ⓒ Ⓓ	32. Ⓐ Ⓑ Ⓒ Ⓓ
5. Ⓐ Ⓑ Ⓒ Ⓓ	12. Ⓐ Ⓑ Ⓒ Ⓓ	19. Ⓐ Ⓑ Ⓒ Ⓓ	26. Ⓐ Ⓑ Ⓒ Ⓓ	33. Ⓐ Ⓑ Ⓒ Ⓓ
6. Ⓐ Ⓑ Ⓒ Ⓓ	13. Ⓐ Ⓑ Ⓒ Ⓓ	20. Ⓐ Ⓑ Ⓒ Ⓓ	27. Ⓐ Ⓑ Ⓒ Ⓓ	34. Ⓐ Ⓑ Ⓒ Ⓓ
7. Ⓐ Ⓑ Ⓒ Ⓓ	14 Ⓐ Ⓑ Ⓒ Ⓓ	21. Ⓐ Ⓑ Ⓒ Ⓓ	28. Ⓐ Ⓑ Ⓒ Ⓓ	35. Ⓐ Ⓑ Ⓒ Ⓓ

CONJUNCTION AND DETERMINERS

LEARNING OBJECTIVES

➤ Conjunctions
➤ Determiners

PRACTICE EXERCISE

1. Fill in the blanks with the suitable conjunction from the options given below.

   It's _________ four o'clock! We will not be late for the flight to Goa.
   (A) already
   (B) than
   (C) only
   (D) which

2. Fill in the blanks with the suitable conjunction from the options given below.

   The house_________ we've just bought overlooks the beach.
   (A) that
   (B) what
   (C) then
   (D) where

3. Fill in the blanks with the suitable conjunction from the options given below.

   _________the night, there was a thunder storm and It shattered the windows,
   (A) In
   (B) Late
   (C) For
   (D) None of these

4. Fill in the blanks with the suitable conjunction from the options given below.

   The children have playing video games on the internet _________ four hours.
   (A) since
   (B) when
   (C) for
   (D) then

5. Fill in the blanks with the suitable conjunction from the options given below.

   I was shocked _________ I saw my picture in the obituary section of the newspaper.
   (A) when
   (B) on
   (C) while
   (D) where

6. Fill in the blanks with the suitable conjunction from the options given below.

   We didn't enjoy our vacations _________ the weather was awful.
   (A) since   (B) however
   (C) because   (D) until

7. Fill in the blanks with the suitable conjunction from the options given below.

_________you had worked a little harder, you would have in your exams!

(A) Only
(B) If
(C) Since
(D) When

8. Fill in the blanks with the suitable conjunction from the options given below.

Sandhya! Please make sure you close all the windows _________ it starts raining.

(A) since
(B) while
(C) for
(D) before

9. Fill in the blanks with the most suitable determiners:

"Would you like_________ Coffee?" my host asked.

(A) some
(B) any
(C) little
(D) much

10. Fill in the blanks with the most suitable determiners:

Rajat bought _________ cheese, but he didn't buy _________ bread.

(A) few, any
(B) some, any
(C) some, some
(D) the, the

11. Fill in the blanks with the most suitable determiners:

There are two books on the table. I haven't read _________of them.

(A) neither
(B) either
(C) each
(D) all

12. Fill in the blanks with the most suitable determiners:

"I'd like to practice my English more, but I have _________ opportunity," said Harshita.

(A) few
(B) a few
(C) little
(D) a little

13. Fill in the blanks with the most suitable determiners:

There was _________ food in the refrigerator. It was nearly empty.

(A) few
(B) a few
(C) little
(D) a little

14. Fill in the blanks with the most suitable determiners:

Lara hasn't got her camera, so she can't take _________ photograph.

(A) some
(B) any
(C) no
(D) either

15. Fill in the blanks with the most suitable determiners:

Richa didn't eat _________ she not hungry

(A) anybody
(B) something
(C) anything
(D) somebody

Fill in the blanks in the given paragraph with articles and determiners the options given below:

Ashoka was____16____emperor of India. He is known as Ashoka____17____Great. He ruled from Pataliputra as____18____capital city of ____19___empire. In his youth, Ashoka waged ____20____battles against____21____ enemies. One of____22____best known invasions was against Kalinga.____23____ battle proved to be ____24____ turning point in____25____life.

16.

   (A) an   B) the

   (C) a   D) some

17.

   (A) a   B) his

   (C) this   D) the

18.

   (A) his   B) the

   (C) a   D) an

19.

   (A) the   (B) his

   (C) an   (D) a

20.

   (A) much   (B) many

   (C) all   (D) a few

21.

   (A) all   (B) both

   (C) his   (D) many

22.

   (A) their   (B) the

   (C) this   (D) that

23.

   (A) This   (B) Their

   (C) All   (D) Both

24.

   (A) a   (B) an

   (C) some   (D) that

25.

   (A) the   (B) his

   (C) a   (D) this

Darken Your Choice with HB Pencil

1.	Ⓐ Ⓑ Ⓒ Ⓓ	6.	Ⓐ Ⓑ Ⓒ Ⓓ	11.	Ⓐ Ⓑ Ⓒ Ⓓ	16	Ⓐ Ⓑ Ⓒ Ⓓ	21.	Ⓐ Ⓑ Ⓒ Ⓓ
2.	Ⓐ Ⓑ Ⓒ Ⓓ	7.	Ⓐ Ⓑ Ⓒ Ⓓ	12.	Ⓐ Ⓑ Ⓒ Ⓓ	17.	Ⓐ Ⓑ Ⓒ Ⓓ	22.	Ⓐ Ⓑ Ⓒ Ⓓ
3.	Ⓐ Ⓑ Ⓒ Ⓓ	8.	Ⓐ Ⓑ Ⓒ Ⓓ	13.	Ⓐ Ⓑ Ⓒ Ⓓ	18.	Ⓐ Ⓑ Ⓒ Ⓓ	23.	Ⓐ Ⓑ Ⓒ Ⓓ
4.	Ⓐ Ⓑ Ⓒ Ⓓ	9.	Ⓐ Ⓑ Ⓒ Ⓓ	14.	Ⓐ Ⓑ Ⓒ Ⓓ	19.	Ⓐ Ⓑ Ⓒ Ⓓ	24.	Ⓐ Ⓑ Ⓒ Ⓓ
5.	Ⓐ Ⓑ Ⓒ Ⓓ	10.	Ⓐ Ⓑ Ⓒ Ⓓ	15.	Ⓐ Ⓑ Ⓒ Ⓓ	20.	Ⓐ Ⓑ Ⓒ Ⓓ	25.	Ⓐ Ⓑ Ⓒ Ⓓ

TENSES

LEARNING OBJECTIVES

➤ Tenses and its various types
➤ Uses of different type of tenses

PRACTICE EXERCISE

I. Fill in the blanks with the correct option.

1. What _____________ for breakfast?
   (A) do you usually have
   (B) are you usually having
   (C) have you usually
   (D) do usually you have

2. My brother _____________ very hard at the moment, because some of his colleagues are off sick.
   (A) works   (B) work
   (C) is working   (D) working

3. What _____________ ?
   (A) mean this word
   (B) means this word
   (C) is this word meaning
   (D) does this word mean

4. Ouch! _____________ on my foot!
   (A) You stand   (B) You're standing
   (C) You are stand (D) You'll stand

5. What _____________ this weekend?
   (A) are you doing (B) do you do
   (C) are you do   (D) are doing

6. What _____________ at the weekend?
   (A) are you normally do
   (B) are you normally doing
   (C) do you normally do
   (D) do you normally doing

7. A: What _____________ ? B: She's an architect.
   (A) is your sister doing
   (B) does your sister do
   (C) does your sister
   (D) is your sister do

8. A: How's your brother? B: He's fine. He _____________ hard at the moment, because he's got his final exams next month.
   (A) studies   (B) is studying
   (C) is study   (D) studys

9. I _____________ your new coat!
   (A) like   (B) am liking
   (C) likes   (D) will like

10. I _____________ this film very much. Can we leave?
    (A) don't enjoy   (B) 'm not enjoying
    (C) do enjoy   (D) enjoying

11. A: Where are my keys? Have you seen them? B: No. You _____________ ! Why don't you keep them in a safe place?
    (A) always lose your keys
    (B) are always losing your keys

12. A: The coffee machine ________________ so we'll have to go to a bar. B: Haven't they fixed it yet?
(A) isn't working   (B) doesn't work

13. A: Rachel's a vegetarian, so we'll have to ask the restaurant to provide a vegetarian menu. B: ________________ fish? A: I don't think so.
(A) Does she eat   (B) Is she eating
(C) Is she eat   (D) Eats she

14. A: ________________ a tie to work? B: No, but we've got an inspection from Head Office today!
(A) Are you always wearing
(B) Do you always wear
(C) Wear you always

15. ________________ a coffee?
(A) Do you want   (B) Are you want
(C) Are you wanting (D) None of these

16. I ________________ tennis every Sunday morning.
(A) playing   (B) play
(C) am playing   (C) am play

17. Don't make so much noise. Noriko ________________ to study for her ESL test!
(A) try   (B) tries
(C) tried   (D) is trying

18. Jun-Sik ________________ his teeth before breakfast every morning.
(A) will cleaned   (B) is cleaning
(C) cleans   (D) clean

19. Sorry, she can't come to the phone. She ________________ a bath!
(A) is having   (B) having
(C) have   (D) has

20. ________________ many times every winter in Frankfurt.
(A) It snows   (B) It snowed
(C) It is snowing   (D) It is snow

21. How many students in your class ________________ from Korea?
(A) comes   (B) come
(C) came   (D) are coming

22. Weather report: "It's seven o'clock in Frankfurt and ________________ ."
(A) there is snow   (B) it's snowing
(C) it snows   (D) it snowed

23. Babies ________________ when they are hungry.
(A) cry   (B) cries
(C) cried   (D) are crying

24. Jane: "What ________________ in the evenings?"
Mary: "Usually I watch TV or read a book."
(A) you doing   (B) you do
(C) do you do   (D) are you doing

25. Jane: "What ________________ ?"
Mary: "I'm trying to fix my calculator."
(A) you doing   (B) you do
(C) do you do   (D) are you doing

26. Jane ________________ her blue jeans today, but usually she wears a skirt or a dress.
(A) wears   (B) wearing
(C) wear   (D) is wearing

27. I think I ________________ a new calculator. This one does not work properly any more.
(A) needs   (A) needed
(B) need   (C) am needing

28. Sorry, you can't borrow my pencil. I ________________ it myself.
(A) was using   (B) using
(C) use   (D) am using

29. At a school dance:
Jane: "________________ yourself?"
Mary: "Yes, I'm having a great time!"
(A) You enjoying
(B) Enjoy you
(C) Do you enjoy
(D) Are you enjoying

30. I've just finished reading a story called Dangerous Game. It's about a man who ________________ his wife because he doesn't want to lose her.
(A) kills   (B) killed
(C) kill   (D) is killing

I. **Direction 31-35:** Fill in the blanks in the given passage using appropriate tense forms from the option that follow:

The old man _____ 31_____ his eyes and for a moment, it looked as if he____32____ back from a long way away. Then he____33_____.

"What_____34_____he asked.

"Supper," said the boy. "We_____35_____ to have supper."

31.
(A) was opening   (B) opened
(C) opens   (D) had opened

32.
(A) was coming   (B) will be coming
(C) is coming   (D) is going to come

33.
(A) smile   (B) smiled
(C) has smiled   (D) will smile

34.
(A) you have got   (B) had you got
(C) you had got   (D) have you got

35.
(A) are going   (B) were going
(C) shall   (D) are

—Darken Your Choice with HB Pencil—

1.	Ⓐ Ⓑ Ⓒ Ⓓ	8.	Ⓐ Ⓑ Ⓒ Ⓓ	15.	Ⓐ Ⓑ Ⓒ Ⓓ	22	Ⓐ Ⓑ Ⓒ Ⓓ	29.	Ⓐ Ⓑ Ⓒ Ⓓ
2.	Ⓐ Ⓑ Ⓒ Ⓓ	9.	Ⓐ Ⓑ Ⓒ Ⓓ	16.	Ⓐ Ⓑ Ⓒ Ⓓ	23.	Ⓐ Ⓑ Ⓒ Ⓓ	30.	Ⓐ Ⓑ Ⓒ Ⓓ
3.	Ⓐ Ⓑ Ⓒ Ⓓ	10.	Ⓐ Ⓑ Ⓒ Ⓓ	17.	Ⓐ Ⓑ Ⓒ Ⓓ	24.	Ⓐ Ⓑ Ⓒ Ⓓ	31.	Ⓐ Ⓑ Ⓒ Ⓓ
4.	Ⓐ Ⓑ Ⓒ Ⓓ	11.	Ⓐ Ⓑ Ⓒ Ⓓ	18.	Ⓐ Ⓑ Ⓒ Ⓓ	25.	Ⓐ Ⓑ Ⓒ Ⓓ	32.	Ⓐ Ⓑ Ⓒ Ⓓ
5.	Ⓐ Ⓑ Ⓒ Ⓓ	12.	Ⓐ Ⓑ Ⓒ Ⓓ	19.	Ⓐ Ⓑ Ⓒ Ⓓ	26.	Ⓐ Ⓑ Ⓒ Ⓓ	33.	Ⓐ Ⓑ Ⓒ Ⓓ
6.	Ⓐ Ⓑ Ⓒ Ⓓ	13.	Ⓐ Ⓑ Ⓒ Ⓓ	20.	Ⓐ Ⓑ Ⓒ Ⓓ	27.	Ⓐ Ⓑ Ⓒ Ⓓ	34.	Ⓐ Ⓑ Ⓒ Ⓓ
7.	Ⓐ Ⓑ Ⓒ Ⓓ	14.	Ⓐ Ⓑ Ⓒ Ⓓ	21.	Ⓐ Ⓑ Ⓒ Ⓓ	28.	Ⓐ Ⓑ Ⓒ Ⓓ	35.	Ⓐ Ⓑ Ⓒ Ⓓ

VOICE AND NARRATION 

LEARNING OBJECTIVES

➤ Active and Passive Voice
➤ Direct and Indirect speech

PRACTICE EXERCISE

I. Fill in the blanks with suitable active and passive verb forms.

1. This house ______________ in 1970 by my grandfather.
   (A) built   (B) was built
   (C) was build   (D) has built

2. The robbers ______________ by the police.
   (A) have arrested
   (B) have been arrested
   (C) was arrested
   (D) had arrested

3. We ______________ for the examination.
   (A) have preparing
   (B) are preparing
   (C) had preparing
   (D) have been prepared

4. It ______________ since yesterday.
   (A) is raining
   (B) has been raining
   (C) have been raining
   (D) was raining

5. I ______________ for five hours.
   (A) have been working
   (B) has been working
   (C) was working
   (D) am working

6. The students ______________ to submit their reports by the end of this week.
   (A) have asked   (B) were asked
   (C) has asked   (D) are asking

7. She ______________ for a while.
   (A) are ailing
   (B) is ailing
   (C) has been ailing
   (D) have been ailing

8. The teacher ______________ the student for lying.
   (A) has been punished
   (B) punished
   (C) is punished
   (D) was punished

9. I ______________ to become a successful writer.
   (A) have always wanted
   (B) am always wanted
   (C) was always wanted
   (D) am always wanting

10. The inmates of the juvenile home ______________ well by their caretakers.
    (A) were not being treated
    (B) were not treating
    (C) have not being treated
    (D) was not being treated

11. As the patient could not walk, he ___________ home in a wheel chair.
(A) has carried
(B) has been carried
(C) was carried
(D) was carrying

12. The injured ___________ to the hospital in an ambulance.
(A) were taking
(B) was taking
(C) were taken
(D) have taken

13. Most of the patient visits ___________ to physician assistants in the recent years all around the world.
(A) have been made
(B) was made
(C) will have been made
(D) have made
(E) make

14. These differences between two photographs ___________ with the help of Photoshop.
(A) should remove
(B) must have removed
(C) have to remove
(D) could have been removed
(E) were able to remove

15. No clinical studies ___________ in this child disease research so far.
(A) had completed
(B) will be completed
(C) have completed
(D) had to complete
(E) have been completed

16. The government ___________ that the tasks ___________ with great success.
(A) is confirming / maintained
(B) confirms / have been maintained
(C) was confirmed / have maintained
(D) will confirm / had been maintained
(E) confirmed / are maintaining

17. With this comprehensive international report, the country's position in the regional and global arena ___________ with measurable criteria.
(A) is to identify
(B) identifies
(C) will be identified
(D) identified
(E) is going to identify

18. The critics ___________ that the review ___________ as a book in English and in many other languages.
(A) are said / could be published
(B) say / can be published
(C) will say / had been published
(D) said / may be published
(E) have said / should publish

19. New legislation ___________ in the congress but it ___________ by many.
(A) was introduced / wasn't accepted
(B) introduced / didn't accept
(C) will be introduced / isn't accepted
(D) introduced / hadn't been accepted
(E) is introduced / won't accept

20. If you would like to know what ___________ in the project so far, you ___________ the full report at our website.
(A) has been completed / may be visited
(B) completed / will be found
(C) completes / should be found
(D) was completed / had been found
(E) will be completed / can find

21. These clothes ___________ for daily use so you ___________ them wherever you want.
(A) design / should be worn
(B) will be designed / must wear
(C) are designed / can wear
(D) were designed / could be worn
(E) designed / might be worn

22. A more developed model of this car _______________ in the showroom soon.
   (A) is going to show
   (B) will be shown
   (C) was shown
   (D) has been shown
   (E) had shown

II. Fill in the blanks with the correct form of verb given in brackets.

23. Paul _______________ (send) to prison. (Future tense)

24. He _______________ (tell) to wait outside. (Past tense)

25. I _______________ (not pay) for the work. (Past tense)

26. Policemen _______________ (often ask) the way. (Present tense)

27. The lawn _______________ (cut) once a week. (Present tense)

28. We _______________ (ask) by the police. (Future tense)

29. They _______________ (teach) French. (Present tense)

30. The fire brigade _______________ (phone) soon after the fire had broken out. (Past tense)

HOTS (ACHIEVERS SECTION)

Six bananas___31___ into a pulp. Half a litre of milk___32___and banana pulp and sugar___33___ to it. The mixture___34___ and then___35___from the heat.

31.
   (A) is crushed
   (B) are crushed
   (C) should crush
   (D) should be crush

32.
   (A) is boiled
   (B) will be boiled
   (C) was boiled
   (D) should boil

33.
   (A) is added
   (B) was added
   (C) are added
   (D) should be adding

34.
   (A) is stirred   (B) will stir
   (C) are stirred   (D) should stir

35.
   (A) was removed
   (B) will be removed
   (C) are removed
   (D) removed

---Darken Your Choice with HB Pencil---

#	A	B	C	D	#	A	B	C	D	#	A	B	C	D	#	A	B	C	D	#	A	B	C	D
1.	Ⓐ	Ⓑ	Ⓒ	Ⓓ	8.	Ⓐ	Ⓑ	Ⓒ	Ⓓ	15.	Ⓐ	Ⓑ	Ⓒ	Ⓓ	22	Ⓐ	Ⓑ	Ⓒ	Ⓓ	29.	Ⓐ	Ⓑ	Ⓒ	Ⓓ
2.	Ⓐ	Ⓑ	Ⓒ	Ⓓ	9.	Ⓐ	Ⓑ	Ⓒ	Ⓓ	16.	Ⓐ	Ⓑ	Ⓒ	Ⓓ	23.	Ⓐ	Ⓑ	Ⓒ	Ⓓ	30.	Ⓐ	Ⓑ	Ⓒ	Ⓓ
3.	Ⓐ	Ⓑ	Ⓒ	Ⓓ	10.	Ⓐ	Ⓑ	Ⓒ	Ⓓ	17.	Ⓐ	Ⓑ	Ⓒ	Ⓓ	24.	Ⓐ	Ⓑ	Ⓒ	Ⓓ	31.	Ⓐ	Ⓑ	Ⓒ	Ⓓ
4.	Ⓐ	Ⓑ	Ⓒ	Ⓓ	11.	Ⓐ	Ⓑ	Ⓒ	Ⓓ	18.	Ⓐ	Ⓑ	Ⓒ	Ⓓ	25.	Ⓐ	Ⓑ	Ⓒ	Ⓓ	32.	Ⓐ	Ⓑ	Ⓒ	Ⓓ
5.	Ⓐ	Ⓑ	Ⓒ	Ⓓ	12.	Ⓐ	Ⓑ	Ⓒ	Ⓓ	19.	Ⓐ	Ⓑ	Ⓒ	Ⓓ	26.	Ⓐ	Ⓑ	Ⓒ	Ⓓ	33.	Ⓐ	Ⓑ	Ⓒ	Ⓓ
6.	Ⓐ	Ⓑ	Ⓒ	Ⓓ	13.	Ⓐ	Ⓑ	Ⓒ	Ⓓ	20.	Ⓐ	Ⓑ	Ⓒ	Ⓓ	27.	Ⓐ	Ⓑ	Ⓒ	Ⓓ	34.	Ⓐ	Ⓑ	Ⓒ	Ⓓ
7.	Ⓐ	Ⓑ	Ⓒ	Ⓓ	14.	Ⓐ	Ⓑ	Ⓒ	Ⓓ	21.	Ⓐ	Ⓑ	Ⓒ	Ⓓ	28.	Ⓐ	Ⓑ	Ⓒ	Ⓓ	35.	Ⓐ	Ⓑ	Ⓒ	Ⓓ

COMPREHENSION

LEARNING OBJECTIVES

➤ Reading Comprehension

PRACTICE EXERCISE

Exercise 1

Read the passages and choose the correct option to answer the questions that follow:

At this stage of civilisation, when many nations are brought in to close and vital contact for good and evil, it is essential, as never before, that their gross ignorance of one another should be diminished, that they should begin to understand a little of one another's historical experience and resulting mentality. It is the fault of the English to expect the people of other countries to react as they do to political and international situations. Our genuine goodwill and good intentions are often brought to nothing, because we expect other people to be like us. This would be corrected if we knew the history, not necessarily in detail but in broad outlines, of the social and political conditions which have given to each nation its present character.

1. According to the author, 'Mentality' of a nation is mainly a product of its

   (A) history

   (B) international position

   (C) politics

   (D) present character

2. The need for a greater understanding between nations

   (A) was always there

   (B) is no longer there

   (C) is more today than ever before

   (D) will always be there

3. The character of a nation is the result of its

   (A) mentality

   (B) cultural heritage

   (C) gross ignorance

   (D) socio-political conditions

4. According to the author, his countrymen should

   (A) read the story of other nations

   (B) have a better understanding of other nations

   (C) not react to other actions

   (D) have vital contacts with other nations

5. Englishmen like others to react to political situations like

   (A) us

   (B) themselves

   (C) others

   (D) each others

Exercise 2

Male lions are rather reticent about expending their energy in hunting; more than three quarters of kills are made by lionesses, who stay in front, tensely scanning ahead, the cubs lag playfully behind and the males bring up the rear, walking slowly, their massive heads nodding with each step as if they were bored with the whole matter. But slothfulness may have survival value. With lionesses busy hunting, the males function as guard for the cubs, protecting them particularly from hyenas.

6. According to the passage, male lions generally do not go for hunting because
    (A) they do not like it
    (B) they want lioness to get training
    (C) they wish to save their vigour for other things
    (D) they are very lazy

7. Male lions protect their cubs
    (A) from the members of their own species
    (B) from hyenas only
    (C) from hyenas as much as from other enemies
    (D) more from hyenas than from other animals

8. Lioness go for hunting
    (A) all alone
    (B) with their male partners only
    (C) with their cubs and male partners
    (D) with their cubs only

9. When the lionesses go in search for their prey, they are very
    (A) serious
    (B) cautious
    (C) playful
    (D) sluggish

10. Which word is the passage means "hesitant"?

    (A) slothfulness
    (B) Reticent
    (C) Lay
    (D) Expend

Exercise 3

What needs to be set right is our approach to work. It is a common sight in our country of employees reporting for duty on time and at the same time doing little work. If an assessment is made of time they spend in gossiping, drinking tea, eating "pan" and smoking cigarettes, it will be shocking to know that the time devoted to actual work is negligible. The problem is the standard, which the leader in administration sets for the staff. Forget the ministers because they mix politics and administration. What do top bureaucrats do? What do the below down officials do? The administration set up remains weak mainly because the employees do not have the right example to follow and they are more concerned about being in the good books of the bosses than doing work.

11. The employees in our country
    (A) are quite punctual but not duty conscious
    (B) are not punctual, but somehow manage to complete their work
    (C) are somewhat lazy but good natured
    (D) are not very highly qualified

12. According to the writer, the administration in India
    (A) is by and large effective
    (B) is very strict and firm
    (C) is affected by red tape
    (D) is more or less ineffective

13. The word 'assessment' means
    (A) enquiry
    (B) report
    (C) evaluation
    (D) summary

14. The leadership in administration

    (A) sets a fine example to the employees

    (B) is of a reasonably high standard

    (C) is composed of idealists

    (D) is of a very poor standard

15. The central idea of passage could be best expressed by the following

    (A) The employee outlook towards work is justified

    (B) The employee must change their outlook towards work

    (C) The employees would never change their work culture

    (D) The employer-employee relationship is far from healthy

Exercise 4

Speech is a great blessing but it can also be a great curse. While it helps us to make our intentions and desires known to our fellows, it can also if we use it carelessly, make our attitude completely misunderstood. A slip of the tongue, the use an of unusual word, or of an ambiguous word, and so on, may create an enemy where we had hoped to win a friend. Again, different classes of people use different vocabularies, and the ordinary speech of an educated may strike an uneducated listener as pompous. Unwillingly, we may use a word which bears a different meaning to our listener from what it does to men of our own class. Thus, speech is not a gift to use lightly without thought, but one which demands careful handling. Only a fool will express himself alike to all kinds of men.

16. The best way to win a friend is to avoid

    (A) irony in speech

    (B) pomposity in speech

    (C) verbosity in speech

    (D) ambiguity in speech

17. While talking to an uneducated person, we should use

    (A) ordinary speech

    (B) his vocabulary

    (C) simple words

    (D) polite language

18. If one used the same style of language with everyone, one would sound

    (A) flat

    (B) boring

    (C) foolish

    (D) democratic

19. A 'slip of the tongue' means something said

    (A) wrongly by choice

    (B) unintentionally

    (C) without giving proper thought

    (D) to hurt another person

20. Speech can be curse, because it can

    (A) hurt others

    (B) lead to carelessness

    (C) create misunderstanding

    (D) reveal our intentions

Exercise 5

Mahatma Gandhi believed that industrialisation was no answer to the problems that plague the mass of India's poor and that villagers should be taught to be self-sufficient in food, weave their own cloth from cotton and eschew the glittering prizes that the 20th century so temptingly offers. Such an idyllic and rural paradise did not appear to those who inherited the reins of political power.

21. The meaning of 'glittering prizes that the 20th century so temptingly offers' is

    (A) pursuit of a commercialised material culture

    (B) replacement of rural by urban interests

    (C) complete removal of poverty

    (D) absence of violence and corruption

22. The basis of 'an idyllic and rural paradise' is
    (A) rapid industrialisation of villages
    (B) self sufficiency in food clothes and simplicity of the lifestyle
    (C) bringing to the villages the glittering prizes of the 20th century
    (D) supporting those holdings powerful political positions

23. Which one of the following best illustrates the relationship between the phrases:
    (i) 'eschew the glittering prizes' and
    (ii) 'idyllic and rural paradise'?
    (A) unless you do (i), you cannot have (ii)
    (B) (i) and (ii) are identical in meaning
    (C) first of all you must have (ii) in order to do (i)

24. Mahatma Gandhi's views opposed industrialisation of villages because
    (A) it would help the poor and not the rich
    (B) it would take away the skill of the villagers
    (C) it would affect the culture of the Indians
    (D) it would undermine self-sufficiency and destroy the beauty of life of the villager

25. Mahatma Gandhi's dream of 'an idyllic and rural paradise' was not shared by
    (A) those who did not believe in the industrialisation of the country
    (B) those who called him the Father of Nation
    (C) those who inherited political powers after independence
    (D) those who believed that villages should be self-sufficient in food and cloth

Exercise 6

Organisations are institutions in which members compete for status and power. They compete for resource of the organisation, for example, finance to expand their own departments, for career advancement and for power to control the activities of others. In pursuit of these aims, groups are formed and sectional interests emerge. As a result, policy decisions may serve the ends of political and career systems rather than those of the concern. In this way, the goals of the organisation may be displaced in favour of sectional interests and individual ambition. These preoccupations sometimes prevent the emergence of organic systems. Many of the electronic firms in a study had recently created research and development departments employing highly qualified and well paid scientists and technicians. Their high pay and expert knowledge were sometimes seen as a threat to the established order of rank, power and privilege. Many senior managers had little knowledge of technicality and possibilities of new developments and electronics. Some felt that close cooperation with the experts in an organic system would reveal their ignorance and show their experience was now redundant.

26. The theme of the passage is
    (A) groupism in organizations
    (B) individual ambitions in organizations
    (C) frustration of senior managers
    (D) emergence of sectional interests in organizations

27. "Organic system" as related to the organization implies its
    (A) growth with the help of expert knowledge
    (B) growth with input from science and technology
    (C) steady all around development
    (D) natural and unimpeded growth

28. Policy decision in organization would involve
    (A) cooperation at all levels in the organization
    (B) modernization of the organization
    (C) attracting highly qualified personnel
    (D) keeping in view the larger objectives of the organizations

29. The author makes out a case for
    (A) organic system
    (B) Research and Development in organisations

    (C) an understanding between senior and middle level executives
    (D) a refresher course for senior managers

30. The author tends to the senior managers as
    (A) ignorant and incompetent
    (B) a little out of step with their work environment
    (C) jealous of their younger colleagues
    (D) robbed of their rank, power and privilege

1.	Ⓐ Ⓑ Ⓒ Ⓓ	7.	Ⓐ Ⓑ Ⓒ Ⓓ	13.	Ⓐ Ⓑ Ⓒ Ⓓ	19	Ⓐ Ⓑ Ⓒ Ⓓ	25.	Ⓐ Ⓑ Ⓒ Ⓓ
2.	Ⓐ Ⓑ Ⓒ Ⓓ	8.	Ⓐ Ⓑ Ⓒ Ⓓ	14.	Ⓐ Ⓑ Ⓒ Ⓓ	20.	Ⓐ Ⓑ Ⓒ Ⓓ	26.	Ⓐ Ⓑ Ⓒ Ⓓ
3.	Ⓐ Ⓑ Ⓒ Ⓓ	9.	Ⓐ Ⓑ Ⓒ Ⓓ	15.	Ⓐ Ⓑ Ⓒ Ⓓ	21.	Ⓐ Ⓑ Ⓒ Ⓓ	27.	Ⓐ Ⓑ Ⓒ Ⓓ
4.	Ⓐ Ⓑ Ⓒ Ⓓ	10.	Ⓐ Ⓑ Ⓒ Ⓓ	16.	Ⓐ Ⓑ Ⓒ Ⓓ	22.	Ⓐ Ⓑ Ⓒ Ⓓ	28.	Ⓐ Ⓑ Ⓒ Ⓓ
5.	Ⓐ Ⓑ Ⓒ Ⓓ	11.	Ⓐ Ⓑ Ⓒ Ⓓ	17.	Ⓐ Ⓑ Ⓒ Ⓓ	23.	Ⓐ Ⓑ Ⓒ Ⓓ	29.	Ⓐ Ⓑ Ⓒ Ⓓ
6.	Ⓐ Ⓑ Ⓒ Ⓓ	12.	Ⓐ Ⓑ Ⓒ Ⓓ	18.	Ⓐ Ⓑ Ⓒ Ⓓ	24.	Ⓐ Ⓑ Ⓒ Ⓓ	30.	Ⓐ Ⓑ Ⓒ Ⓓ

SPOKEN AND WRITTEN EXPRESSIONS; PUNCTUATION

LEARNING OBJECTIVES

➤ Use of different Punctuation marks

PRACTICE EXERCISE

I. **Add commas wherever required in the following sentences.**

1. After a hard day at the office I like to relax with a large gin.

2. The recipe needed jam flour sugar fruit eggs ketchup and baking powder.

3. "Look at this" he whispered.

4. Paulina his wife of many years had decided to go and live in Greece.

5. As the sun began to sink over the sea Karen got ready to go out.

6. She was intelligent not especially practical.

7. The thief was wearing impractical high heels so she could not run fast.

8. We go to Blackpool for the cuisine not the weather.

9. "I advise you" said the teacher "not to cross me again today."

10. Steven his head still spinning walked out of the office for the last time.

II. **Decide which pairs of clauses can be connected with a semi-colon in the following sentences.**

11. Which can/should be connected with a semi-colon?

    (A) I hate rice pudding _____ dairy products don't agree with me.

    (B) Spain is lovely _____ hot weather and friendly people.

    (C) Spain _____ lovely beaches, endless blue sea and great weather.

    (D) Spain is a lovely country _____ the beaches are endless and the weather is always good.

12. Which can/should be connected with a semi-colon?

    (A) Paris is a beautiful city _____ wide streets and sunshine.

    (B) Havana is a lovely city _____ rice pudding is one of my favourite foods.

    (C) I would love to go to France _____ Paris is a lovely city.

    (D) I would love to go to Greece _____ I love ancient history.

13. Which can/should be connected with a semi-colon?

   (A) Gran hates going to bed early _______ there is too much on the telly.

   (B) Gran hates doing DIY _______ too much like hard work.

   (C) Gran hates going to bed early _______ the wallpaper in her house is peeling.

   (D) Gran hates doing DIY _______ the wallpaper in her house is peeling.

14. Which can/should be connected with a semi-colon?

   (A) Understanding grammar is very important _______ despite its complexity.

   (B) Understanding grammar is very important _______ clear communication is an essential skill.

   (C) Understanding grammar is very important _______ most high level jobs require good writing skills.

   (D) Understanding grammar is very important _______ although it is not always the most fascinating subject on the planet.

15. Which can/should be connected with a semi-colon?

   (A) The stock exchange fell sharply _______ investor confidence is very low.

   (B) The stock exchange fell sharply _______ many investors decided to sell their shares.

   (C) The stock exchange fell sharply _______ a difficult day for everybody.

   (D) The stock exchange fell sharply _______ I would wait before selling your shares.

III. Select the sentence which is correctly punctuated.

16. (A) Spain is a beautiful country; the beaches are warm, sandy and spotlessly clean.

   (B) Spain is a beautiful country: the beaches are warm, sandy and spotlessly clean.

   (C) Spain is a beautiful country, the beaches are warm, sandy and spotlessly clean.

   (D) Spain is a beautiful country; the beaches are warm, sandy and spotlessly clean.

17. (A) The children's books were all left in the following places: Mrs. Smith's room, Mr. Powell's office and the caretaker's cupboard.

   (B) The children's books were all left in the following places; Mrs. Smith's room, Mr. Powell's office and the caretaker's cupboard.

   (C) The children's books were all left in the following places: Mrs. Smiths room, Mr. Powell's office and the caretakers cupboard.

   (D) The children's books were all left in the following places, Mrs. Smith's room, Mr. Powell's office and the caretaker's cupboard.

18. (A) She always enjoyed sweets, chocolate, marshmallows and toffee apples.

   (B) She always enjoyed: sweets, chocolate, marshmallows and toffee apples.

   (C) She always enjoyed sweets chocolate marshmallows and toffee apples.

   (D) She always enjoyed sweet's, chocolate, marshmallow's and toffee apple's.

19. (A) Sarah's uncle's car was found without its wheels in that old derelict warehouse.

(B) Sarah's uncle's car was found without its wheels in that old, derelict warehouse.

(C) Sarah's uncles car was found without its wheels in that old, derelict warehouse.

(D) Sarah's uncle's car was found without its wheel's in that old, derelict warehouse.

20. (A) I can't see Tim's car, there must have been an accident.

(B) I can't see Tims car; there must have been an accident.

(C) I can't see Tim's car there must have been an accident.

(D) I can't see Tim's car; there must have been an accident.

21. (A) Paul's neighbours were terrible; so his brother's friends went round to have a word.

(B) Paul's neighbours were terrible: so his brother's friends went round to have a word.

(C) Paul's neighbours were terrible, so his brother's friends went round to have a word.

(D) Paul's neighbours were terrible so his brother's friends went round to have a word.

22. (A) Tim's gran, a formidable woman, always bought him chocolate, cakes, sweets and a nice fresh apple.

(B) Tim's gran a formidable woman always bought him chocolate, cakes, sweets, and a nice fresh apple.

(C) Tim's gran, a formidable woman, always bought him chocolate cakes sweets and a nice fresh apple.

(D) Tim's gran, a formidable woman, always bought him chocolate, cakes, sweets and a nice fresh apple.

23. (A) After stealing Tims car, the thief lost his way and ended up the chief constable's garage.

(B) After stealing Tim's car the thief lost his way and ended up the chief constable's garage.

(C) After stealing Tim's car, the thief lost his way and ended up the chief constable's garage.

(D) After stealing Tim's car, the thief lost his' way and ended up the chief constable's garage.

24. (A) We decided to visit: Spain, Greece, Portugal and Italy's mountains.

(B) We decided to visit Spain, Greece, Portugal and Italys mountains.

(C) We decided to visit Spain, Greece, Portugal and Italy's mountains.

(D) We decided to visit Spain Greece Portugal and Italy's mountains.

25. (A) That tall man, Paul's grandad, is this month's winner.

(B) That tall man Paul's grandad is this month's winner.

(C) That tall man, Paul's grandad, is this months winner.

(D) That tall man, Pauls grandad, is this month's winner.

V. Use appropriate punctuation marks in the following sentences.

26. We had a great time in France the kids really enjoyed it

27. Some people work best in the mornings others do better in the evenings

28. What are you doing next weekend

29. Mother had to go into hospital she had heart problems

30. Did you understand why I was upset

Direction 1-2: Select options for correctly ending the given sentences.

31. If you have any doubts could you please speak now
    (A) Comma
    (B) full stop
    (C) Exclamation mark
    (D) question mark

32. Khan was angry and shouted at his son, "Go to your room now!
    (A) Comma
    (B) Double quotation
    (C) Full stop
    (D) Question mark

Direction 33-35: Select the option correctly showing the number of exclamation marks/ commas required in the following sentence.

33. "Help" she cried. "I can't swim"
    (A) One   (B) two
    (B) Three   (D) None

34. I am taking English Maths and Science at A level and my teacher Ms. Roja believes I should get 3As.
    (A) None   (B) two
    (C) Four   (D) three

35. She bought milk eggs and bread.
    (A) Two   (B) three
    (C) One   (D) none

Darken Your Choice with HB Pencil

1. Ⓐ Ⓑ Ⓒ Ⓓ	8. Ⓐ Ⓑ Ⓒ Ⓓ	15. Ⓐ Ⓑ Ⓒ Ⓓ	22 Ⓐ Ⓑ Ⓒ Ⓓ	29. Ⓐ Ⓑ Ⓒ Ⓓ
2. Ⓐ Ⓑ Ⓒ Ⓓ	9. Ⓐ Ⓑ Ⓒ Ⓓ	16. Ⓐ Ⓑ Ⓒ Ⓓ	23. Ⓐ Ⓑ Ⓒ Ⓓ	30. Ⓐ Ⓑ Ⓒ Ⓓ
3. Ⓐ Ⓑ Ⓒ Ⓓ	10. Ⓐ Ⓑ Ⓒ Ⓓ	17. Ⓐ Ⓑ Ⓒ Ⓓ	24. Ⓐ Ⓑ Ⓒ Ⓓ	31. Ⓐ Ⓑ Ⓒ Ⓓ
4. Ⓐ Ⓑ Ⓒ Ⓓ	11. Ⓐ Ⓑ Ⓒ Ⓓ	18. Ⓐ Ⓑ Ⓒ Ⓓ	25. Ⓐ Ⓑ Ⓒ Ⓓ	32. Ⓐ Ⓑ Ⓒ Ⓓ
5. Ⓐ Ⓑ Ⓒ Ⓓ	12. Ⓐ Ⓑ Ⓒ Ⓓ	19. Ⓐ Ⓑ Ⓒ Ⓓ	26. Ⓐ Ⓑ Ⓒ Ⓓ	33. Ⓐ Ⓑ Ⓒ Ⓓ
6. Ⓐ Ⓑ Ⓒ Ⓓ	13. Ⓐ Ⓑ Ⓒ Ⓓ	20. Ⓐ Ⓑ Ⓒ Ⓓ	27. Ⓐ Ⓑ Ⓒ Ⓓ	34. Ⓐ Ⓑ Ⓒ Ⓓ
7. Ⓐ Ⓑ Ⓒ Ⓓ	14. Ⓐ Ⓑ Ⓒ Ⓓ	21. Ⓐ Ⓑ Ⓒ Ⓓ	28. Ⓐ Ⓑ Ⓒ Ⓓ	35. Ⓐ Ⓑ Ⓒ Ⓓ

MODEL TEST PAPER

Direction (1-2) : Choose the most suitable word/phrase for each blank.

1. I had not met her for a long time, but today suddenly I _________________ her at the shopping mall.
   (A) Ran into
   (B) Ran over
   (C) Ran by
   (D) Ran up

2. That shop is really expensive. They always try to _________________ the customer.
   (A) Rip off
   (B) Rip up
   (C) Rip away
   (D) Rip apart

3. Choose the correct spelling.
   (A) Supercede
   (B) Superceed
   (C) Supersede
   (D) Superseed

4. Select the correct phrase.
   (A) Cry over split milk
   (B) Cry and spill milk
   (C) Cry over split water
   (D) Cry over milk

Direction (5-6) : Fill in the blanks with suitable option.

5. I am not able to take any more printouts _________________
   (A) the printer broke down
   (B) printer breaks down
   (C) as the printer has broken down
   (D) broken down printer it is

6. I've already started from my office and should reach your place _____________
   (A) by 6 pm
   (B) on 6 pm
   (C) at 6 pm
   (D) after 6 pm

7. Read the sentences given below and find the error.
   (A) Although Denise
   (B) had some doubts,
   (C) she found the courses very useful
   (D) No error

Direction (8-10) : Read the passage given below and answer the questions that follow.

It happened over 300 years ago in Holland. Anton van Leeuwenhoek (AN-tun van LAY-vun-hook) had a new microscope that he had made. One day he looked through it at a drop of lake water. What he saw surprised him.

The water was alive with what Leeuwenhoek called "wee beasties." The microscope made tiny organisms look 200 times larger than life size. Leeuwenhoek was one of the first scientists to see living things that were that small. His work was a giant step for science.

Today, microscopes are much stronger. An electron microscope can make tiny organisms look 200,000 times life size. A few electron microscopes can see individual atoms. Pictures can be made to show the objects or organisms much bigger. The pictures add greatly to what we know about tiny objects and organisms. Microscopes have come a long way in 300 years!

8. Leeuwenhoek was surprised to see
   - (A) living things with the microscope
   - (B) he had taken a giant step in science
   - (C) such small living things for the first time
   - (D) tiny organisms 200 times

9. Electron microscopes are much advanced because
   - (A) they can see tiny organisms
   - (B) they can see individual atoms
   - (C) they help us to make pictures
   - (D) they help us see the smallest of objects and organisms, and know about them

10. The main focus of the passage is on
    - (A) microscopes and how they are made
    - (B) Anton van Leeuwenhoek
    - (C) how the discovery of microscope has helped us know about the tiny objects and organisms.
    - (D) how we can make pictures based on the images microscopes see.

Direction (11-13): Choose the most suitable sentence to complete the paragraph.

11. Interviewer: What is three times seven?

    Ron: Twenty-two.

    Interviewer: It's twenty-one. We will still offer you the job as ________
    - (A) you have the courage to give a wrong answer.
    - (B) you are the closest to the actual answer.
    - (C) we like your answer.
    - (D) your clothes are very nice.

12. Don: What was that clicking sound?

    Jane: ________________________

    Lisa: Oh! I didn't see you pressing your car remote-control device.
    - (A) I don't know!
    - (B) Do you really need to know everything?
    - (C) It was just the doors unlocking!
    - (D) Oops! Did you hear a sound?

13. Sentence 1: Even though kettlebell training has been around for a long time, it seems that the popularity of this type of training is at an all time high..

    Sentence 2: ________________________

    Sentence 3: Kettlebells are used to perform ballistic exercises that combine cardiovascular, strength and flexibility training.
    - (A) We have created a huge database of kettlebell exercises with photos and instructional tips to use them effectively!
    - (B) A kettlebell is a cast iron weight that looks a little like a cannonball or a bowling ball with a handle attached to it.
    - (C) Position the kettlebell on the ground between your feet. Explode up while raising the kettlebell to the top position.
    - (D) Keep reading about an exercise you should probably already be doing.

Direction (14-15): Choose the best word to complete the sentence.

14. I don't like walking alone _________ nights as I am _________ scared of the dark.

    (A) throughout, to   (B) over, too

    (C) at, very   (D) in, so

15. The student refused _________ although the teacher insisted again and again.

    (A) answer question

    (B) to question answer

    (C) to answer the question

    (D) answering question

---

1. Ⓐ Ⓑ Ⓒ Ⓓ	4. Ⓐ Ⓑ Ⓒ Ⓓ	7. Ⓐ Ⓑ Ⓒ Ⓓ	10. Ⓐ Ⓑ Ⓒ Ⓓ	13. Ⓐ Ⓑ Ⓒ Ⓓ
2. Ⓐ Ⓑ Ⓒ Ⓓ	5. Ⓐ Ⓑ Ⓒ Ⓓ	8. Ⓐ Ⓑ Ⓒ Ⓓ	11. Ⓐ Ⓑ Ⓒ Ⓓ	14. Ⓐ Ⓑ Ⓒ Ⓓ
3. Ⓐ Ⓑ Ⓒ Ⓓ	6. Ⓐ Ⓑ Ⓒ Ⓓ	9. Ⓐ Ⓑ Ⓒ Ⓓ	12. Ⓐ Ⓑ Ⓒ Ⓓ	15. Ⓐ Ⓑ Ⓒ Ⓓ

HINTS AND SOLUTIONS

1. SYNONYMS, ANTONYMS, HOMONYMS AND HOMOPHONES

Answer Key

1. (A)	2. (B)	3. (C)	4. (C)	5. (A)	6. (C)	7. (D)	8. (A)	9. (D)	10. (A)
11. (B)	12. (D)	13. (A)	14. (D)	15. (C)	16. (C)	17. (A)	18. (D)	19. (B)	20. (A)
20. (C)	21. (C)	23. (A)	24. (D)	25. (D)	26. (B)	27. (A)	28. (B)	29. (D)	30. (A)

HOTS (ACHIEVERS SECTION)

31. (B)	32. (D)	33. (A)	34. (D)

5. What looks like a convenient shortcut may prove to be very inconvenient in the long run.

2. SPELLINGS, ANALOGY AND COLLOCATIONS

Answer Key

1. (B)	2. (B)	3. (C)	4. (D)	5. (D)	6. (B)	7. (B)	8. (C)	9. (B)	10. (C)
11. (A)	12. (B)	13. (A)	14. (C)	15. (A)	16. (A)	17. (B)	18. (D)	19. (C)	20. (C)
21. (A)	22. (B)	23. (B)	24. (A)	25. (B)	26. (D)	27. (B)	28. (D)	29. (A)	30. (A)

HOTS (ACHIEVERS SECTION)

31. (D)	32. (D)	33. (D)	34. (C)	35. (C)

3. ONE WORD AND IDIOMS

Answer Key

1. (C)	2. (B)	3. (C)	4. (D)	5. (A)	6. (C)	7. (D)	8. (C)	9. (A)	10. (C)
11. (B)	12. (D)	13. (B)	14. (B)	15. (D)	16. (A)	17. (A)	18. (C)	19. (B)	20. (B)
21. (D)	22. (A)	23. (B)	24. (B)	25. (B)	26. (B)	27. (C)	28. (C)	29. (A)	30. (A)

HOTS (ACHIEVERS SECTION)

31. (B)	32. (D)	33. (B)	34. (B)	35. (A)

Answer Key

1. (D)	2. (D)	3. (B)	4. (C)	5. (A)	6. (C)	7. (C)	8. (A)	9. (B)	10. (C)

1. (D)

There is no error in this sentence. Basically what the sentence is saying is that 'the comments made by the subject are theories and necessarily connects with the realities.' Since 'comments' is plural, the verb 'show' is correct. So option D is correct.

2. (D)

The Error is in Part D of the sentence. The word loosing here is wrong. There are two distinct words. One is "lose" and other is "loose." Lose means "become unable to find or be deprived of or cease to have or retain something." Loose means "not firmly or tightly fixed in place or detached or able to be detached." While lose is the opposite of find, loose is the opposite of tight. Here the correct word is 'losing.'

3. (B)

The Error is in Part B of the sentence. Here the verb must be placed considering "attention" which is singular whether it is an individual's attention or the whole world's. So the verb must be "was" not "were." So option c is correct.

4. (C)

The Error is in Part C of the sentence. Mumbai Airport is a place. Therefore we can't use "when." When is used for time, where is used for place. So option d is correct.

5. (A)

When a sentence starts with, 'if' it is either imaginative or an assumption. In such cases, we must always use "were." So it should be "If there were less." So option a is correct.

6. (C)

The error lies in part C of the sentence where the preposition 'on' after the verb 'hold' is incorrect as it conveys a different meaning. The correct preposition here would be 'down' and it should read as: 'beautiful and hold down full-time jobs'.

7. (C)

The error lies in part C of the sentence where the preposition 'of' is missing before the word 'whether' as when we use regardless there comes a question regardless of what? And so it should read as: 'regardless of whether the products.'

8. (A)

The error lies in part A of the sentence where the article 'the' before the word 'relaxation' is not required and needs to be omitted. The addition of 'the' before it unnecessary makes it specific noun which is not required. It should read as: 'Fields which requires relaxation in FDI restrictions.'

9. (B)

The error lies in part B of the sentence where the use of past tense for 'cross' is incorrect as it is not in parallel with 'arises'. Thus the correct form is 'when the dramatization crosses the line'

10. (C)

The error lies in part C of the sentence where the pronoun 'his' is missing before the noun 'willingness' which makes it incorrect. The pronoun 'his' is necessary here as it represents the correct subject about whose willingness it is spoken. It should read as: 'has shown his willingness to talk'.

11. Many peoples attended the funeral of the great man.
12. The shepherd took the cattles to the field.
13. Sita could not understands what the teacher was saying.
14. Do you know the importance for clean water?
15. Laugh is the best medicines.
16. The flock of sheeps blocked the road.
17. The children was playing in the Giant's garden.
18. The children decided to surprise Miss Holmes on teacher's day.
19. I saw Richard when I'm on the flight.
20. Man have depended on nature for a long time.
21. Ramu is a honest man.
22. Bread and butter are Sheldon's favourite breakfast.
23. Birds of feathers flock together.
24. The teacher called me on 12 o'clock.
25. The sweets was distributed between all the children.

HOTS (ACHIEVERS SECTION)

My little sister Lisa was practicing how to **ride** a bicycle yesterday. Suddenly I heard a loud crash and ran to see what had happened. I saw that she was lying **on** the ground. I quickly pulled her up and brought her home. She was crying out loud. I quickly **went** inside the house and brought the first aid box. After cleaning the wound, I **applied** antiseptic to the wound. Lisa **had** scratches on her hand and knee. To calm her down, I took her to the nearby shop and bought her a big chocolate. Seeing her favourite chocolate, she immediately **stopped** crying. Within two **days**, her wounds healed, and she went to play again.

5. NOUN

Answer Key

1. Common	2. Common	3. Proper	4. Common	5. Proper
6. Proper	7. Common	8. Proper	9. Proper	10. Common
11. Uncountable	12. Uncountable	13. Countable	14. Uncountable	15. Countable
16. Countable	17. Uncountable	18. Countable	19. Countable	20. Uncountable

HOTS (ACHIEVERS SECTION)

21. Permission	22. Belief	23. Improvement	24. Information	25. Happiness

Answer Key

1. (A)	2. (D)	3. (D)	4. (A)	5. (C)	6. (C)	7. (A)	8. (C)	9. (A)	10. (C)
11. (B)	12. (C)	13. (D)	14. (C)	15. (B)	16. (D)	17. (B)	18. (C)	19. (D)	20. (B)
21. (A)	22. (C)	23. (A)	24. (C)	25. (A)	26. (B)	27. (B)	28. (C)	29. (D)	30. (B)

1. **(A)** Always
2. **(D)** Seldom
3. **(C)** Seldom
4. **(A)** Always
5. **(C)** Never
6. **(C)** Always
7. **(A)** Never
8. **(C)** Never
9. **(A)** Never
10. **(C)** Seldom
11. **(B)** on
12. **(C)** in
13. **(D)** down
14. **(C)** up
15. **(B)** for
16. **(D)** after
17. **(B)** up
18. **(C)** back
19. **(D)** forward
20. **(B)** on
21. **(A)** dropped off
22. **(C)** play down
23. **(A)** come across
24. **(C)** cut back on
25. **(A)** do it over
26. **(B)** left out
27. **(B)** call off
28. **(C)** add up to
29. **(D)** put off
30. **(B)** broken in

HOTS (ACHIEVERS SECTION)

31. (A)	32. (C)	33. (C)	34. (A)	35. (C)

7. ADJECTIVE

Answer Key

1. Heavy – adjective of quality	2. Several – indefinite numeral adjective
3. Faithful – adjective of quality; its – possessive adjective	4. Every – distributive numeral adjective; his – possessive adjective
5. Few – indefinite numeral adjective	6. Neither – distributive numeral adjective
7. Which – interrogative adjective	8. Long – adjective of quality; cold – adjective of quality
9. Every – distributive numeral adjective	10. Several – indefinite numeral adjective
11. prettier	12. Nice
13. most intelligent	14. well
15. biggest	16. big
17. bigger	18. most interesting
19. smarter	20. shorter

HOTS (ACHIEVERS SECTION)

21. careful	22. fluent	23. complete	24. serious	25. sudden

Answer Key

1. (C)	2. (A)	3. (A)	4. (C)	5. (B)	6. (C)	7. (A)	8. (C)	9. (B)	10. (A)
11. (B)	12. (C)	13. (B)	14. (C)	15. (A)	16. (C)	17. (B)	18. (A)	19. (A)	20. (C)
21. (C)	22. (B)	23. (D)	24. (A)	25. (B)	26. (C)	27. (B)	28. (D)	29. (B)	30. (A)

1. **(C)** on
2. **(A)** opposite
3. **(A)** under
4. **(C)** on
5. **(B)** between
6. **(C)** in front of
7. **(A)** behind
8. **(C)** next to
9. **(B)** opposite
10. **(A)** in
11. **(B)** between
12. **(C)** under
13. **(B)** in
14. **(C)** in front of
15. **(A)** above
16. **(C)** behind
17. **(B)** next to
18. **(A)** on
19. **(A)** between
20. **(C)** on
21. **(C)** with
22. **(B)** in
23. **(D)** to
24. **(A)** for
25. **(B)** between
26. **(C)** with
27. **(B)** with
28. **(D)** for
29. **(B)** in
30. **(A)** from

HOTS (ACHIEVERS SECTION)

31. the, the	32. an	33. a	34. a	35. The

Answer Key

1. (C)	2. (A)	3. (A)	4. (C)	5. (A)	6. (C)	7. (B)	8. (D)	9. (A)	10. (B)
11. (B)	12. (C)	13. (C)	14. (B)	15. (C)					

HOTS (ACHIEVERS SECTION)

16. (A)	17. (D)	18. (B)	19. (B)	20. (B)	21. (C)	22. (B)	23. (A)	24. (A)	25. (B)

Answer Key

1. (A)	2. (C)	3. (D)	4. (B)	5. (A)	6. (C)	7. (A)	8. (B)	9. (A)	10. (B)
11. (A)	12. (A)	13. (A)	14. (B)	15. (A)	16. (B)	17. (D)	18. (C)	19. (A)	20. (A)
21. (B)	22. (B)	23. (A)	24. (C)	25. (D)	26. (D)	27. (B)	28. (D)	29. (D)	30. (A)

1. **(A)** do you usually have
2. **(C)** is working
3. **(D)** does this word mean
4. **(B)** You're standing
5. **(A)** are you doing
6. **(C)** do you normally do
7. **(A)** is your sister doing
8. **(B)** is studying
9. **(A)** like
10. **(B)** 'm not enjoying
11. **(A)** always lose your keys
12. **(A)** isn't working
13. **(A)** Does she eat
14. **(B)** Do you always wear
15. **(A)** Do you want
16. **(B)** play
17. **(D)** is trying
18. **(C)** cleans
19. **(A)** is having
20. **(A)** It snows
21. **(B)** come
22. **(B)** it`s snowing
23. **(A)** cry
24. **(C)** do you do
25. **(D)** are you doing
26. **(D)** is wearing
27. **(B)** needed
28. **(D)** am using
29. **(D)** Are you enjoying
30. **(A)** kills

HOTS (ACHIEVERS SECTION)

| 31. (B) | 32. (A) | 33. (B) | 34. (D) | 35. (A) |

11. VOICE AND NARRATION

Answer Key

1. (B)	2. (B)	3. (B)	4. (B)	5. (A)	6. (B)	7. (C)	8. (B)	9. (A)	10. (A)
11. (C)	12. (C)	13. (A)	14. (D)	15. (E)	16. (B)	17. (C)	18. (B)	19. (A)	20. (E)
21. (C)	22. (B)								

23. will be sent	24. was told	25. was not paid	26. are often asked		27. is cut
28. will be asked	29. are taught	30. was phoned			

12. COMPREHENSION

Answer Key

1. (A)	2. (C)	3. (D)	4. (B)	5. (B)	6. (C)	7. (D)	8. (C)	9. (B)	10. (B)
11. (A)	12. (D)	13. (C)	14. (D)	15. (B)	16. (D)	17. (B)	18. (C)	19. (C)	20. (C)
21. (A)	22. (B)	23. (D)	24. (B)	25. (A)	26. (D)	27. (B)	28. (C)	29. (A)	30. (A)

OLYMPIAD WORKBOOK (IEO) CLASS– 10

Answer Key

1. After a hard day at the office, I like to relax with a large gin.	2. The recipe needed jam, flour, sugar, fruit, eggs, ketchup and baking powder.
3. "Look at this," he whispered.	4. Paulina, his wife of many years, had decided to go and live in Greece.
5. As the sun began to sink over the sea, Karen got ready to go out.	6. She was intelligent, not especially practical.
7. The thief was wearing impractical high heels, so she could not run fast.	8. We go to Blackpool for the cuisine, not the weather.
9. "I advise you," said the teacher, "not to cross me again today."	10. Steven, his head still spinning, walked out of the office for the last time.

11. B, C	12. A, B	13. B, C	14. A, D	15. C					
16. (D)	17. (A)	18. (A)	19. (B)	20. (D)	21. (C)	22. (D)	23. (C)	24. (C)	25. (A)

26. We had a great time in France – the kids really enjoyed it.	29. Some people work best in the mornings; others do better in the evenings.
27. What are you doing next weekend?	30. Mother had to go into hospital: she had heart problems.
28. Did you understand why I was upset?	

MODEL TEST PAPER

Answer Key

1. (A)	2. (A)	3. (C)	4. (A)	5. (C)	6. (A)	7. (C)	8. (D)	9. (B)	10. (C)
11. (A)	12. (C)	13. (B)	14. (C)	15. (C)					

SAMPLE OMR ANSWER SHEET

1. STUDENT NAME (IN ENGLISH CAPITAL LETTERS ONLY)

Students must write and darken the respective circles completely using HB Pencil only. Othewise their Answer Sheets will not be evaluated.

PERSONAL DETAILS

2. SCHOOL CODE

3. CLASS

4. SECTION

5. ROLL NO.

6. QUESTION PAPER SET

A ○
B ○
C ○
D ○

7. MOBILE NUMBER

8. GENDER

MALE ○
FEMALE ○

9. STREAM
(Only for Class XI and XII Students)

MATHEMATICS ○
BIOLOGY ○
OTHERS ○

MARK YOUR ANSWERS

1.	Ⓐ Ⓑ Ⓒ Ⓓ	26.	Ⓐ Ⓑ Ⓒ Ⓓ
2.	Ⓐ Ⓑ Ⓒ Ⓓ	27.	Ⓐ Ⓑ Ⓒ Ⓓ
3.	Ⓐ Ⓑ Ⓒ Ⓓ	28.	Ⓐ Ⓑ Ⓒ Ⓓ
4.	Ⓐ Ⓑ Ⓒ Ⓓ	29.	Ⓐ Ⓑ Ⓒ Ⓓ
5.	Ⓐ Ⓑ Ⓒ Ⓓ	30.	Ⓐ Ⓑ Ⓒ Ⓓ
6.	Ⓐ Ⓑ Ⓒ Ⓓ	31.	Ⓐ Ⓑ Ⓒ Ⓓ
7.	Ⓐ Ⓑ Ⓒ Ⓓ	32.	Ⓐ Ⓑ Ⓒ Ⓓ
8.	Ⓐ Ⓑ Ⓒ Ⓓ	33.	Ⓐ Ⓑ Ⓒ Ⓓ
9.	Ⓐ Ⓑ Ⓒ Ⓓ	34.	Ⓐ Ⓑ Ⓒ Ⓓ
10.	Ⓐ Ⓑ Ⓒ Ⓓ	35.	Ⓐ Ⓑ Ⓒ Ⓓ
11.	Ⓐ Ⓑ Ⓒ Ⓓ	36.	Ⓐ Ⓑ Ⓒ Ⓓ
12.	Ⓐ Ⓑ Ⓒ Ⓓ	37.	Ⓐ Ⓑ Ⓒ Ⓓ
13.	Ⓐ Ⓑ Ⓒ Ⓓ	38.	Ⓐ Ⓑ Ⓒ Ⓓ
14.	Ⓐ Ⓑ Ⓒ Ⓓ	39.	Ⓐ Ⓑ Ⓒ Ⓓ
15.	Ⓐ Ⓑ Ⓒ Ⓓ	40.	Ⓐ Ⓑ Ⓒ Ⓓ
16.	Ⓐ Ⓑ Ⓒ Ⓓ	41.	Ⓐ Ⓑ Ⓒ Ⓓ
17.	Ⓐ Ⓑ Ⓒ Ⓓ	42.	Ⓐ Ⓑ Ⓒ Ⓓ
18.	Ⓐ Ⓑ Ⓒ Ⓓ	43.	Ⓐ Ⓑ Ⓒ Ⓓ
19.	Ⓐ Ⓑ Ⓒ Ⓓ	44.	Ⓐ Ⓑ Ⓒ Ⓓ
20.	Ⓐ Ⓑ Ⓒ Ⓓ	45.	Ⓐ Ⓑ Ⓒ Ⓓ
21.	Ⓐ Ⓑ Ⓒ Ⓓ	46.	Ⓐ Ⓑ Ⓒ Ⓓ
22.	Ⓐ Ⓑ Ⓒ Ⓓ	47.	Ⓐ Ⓑ Ⓒ Ⓓ
23.	Ⓐ Ⓑ Ⓒ Ⓓ	48.	Ⓐ Ⓑ Ⓒ Ⓓ
24.	Ⓐ Ⓑ Ⓒ Ⓓ	49.	Ⓐ Ⓑ Ⓒ Ⓓ
25.	Ⓐ Ⓑ Ⓒ Ⓓ	50.	Ⓐ Ⓑ Ⓒ Ⓓ

Signature of the Student & Date of Examination

Signature of the Invigilator & Date of Examination